Ootlin

JENNI FAGAN

Ootlin

A Memoir

HUTCHINSON
HEINEMANN

1 3 5 7 9 10 8 6 4 2

Hutchinson Heinemann
20 Vauxhall Bridge Road
London SW1V 2SA

Hutchinson Heinemann is part of the Penguin Random House
group of companies whose addresses can be found at
global.penguinrandomhouse.com

Penguin
Random House
UK

First published by Hutchinson Heinemann in 2024

www.penguin.co.uk

A CIP catalogue record for this book is available from the British Library.

ISBN 9781529153071 (Hardback)
ISBN 9781529153088 (Trade paperback)

Typeset in 12/14.75 pt Dante MT Std
by Integra Software Services Pvt. Ltd, Pondicherry

Printed and bound in Great Britain by Clays Ltd, Elcograf S.p.A.

The authorised representative in the EEA is Penguin Random House Ireland,
Morrison Chambers, 32 Nassau Street, Dublin D02 YH68

www.greenpenguin.co.uk

Penguin Random House is committed to a sustainable future for
our business, our readers and our planet. This book is made from
Forest Stewardship Council® certified paper.

MIX
Paper | Supporting
responsible forestry
FSC
www.fsc.org   FSC® C018179

For all those who traverse
the underworld
on nothing more than a feather

Tell your own story and you
will be interesting.

Louise Bourgeois

You think your pain and your
heartbreak are unprecedented
in the history of the world,
but then you read.

James Baldwin

There is always a story before the story and this first one, too, starts long after it all begins.

Prologue

This is a story about stories. The stories we are told about who we are by others.

Twenty years ago I began writing this memoir as a suicide note and as I was trying for hours to sum up my life in one small letter all I could think was – is that it?

This note said so little about me and in no way captured the life that had brought me to that exact moment. It was incredibly sad to think a small assemblage of words might be all I had to leave behind, so I decided before I went I should look at my entire life just once – a story so much bigger than me.

I borrowed a typewriter from a neighbour. For the next few weeks I typed for fourteen hours a day on a tiny tabletop on the floor, that I had found in the street. I smoked and drank coffee endlessly in my tiny housing association flat, until one night I placed down a full stop to find I had a full manuscript. After I had written 'The End' I locked the entire typed-up document away in a flight case and vowed never to look at it again, or discuss its contents with anyone.

In one decisive act I had taken what was a suicide note and turned it into a book that kept me alive for many more decades.

Returning to stories, we hear them in every aspect of life, on the bus, in school, at home, the pub, in our relationships, via every single aspect of human culture this one shared constant underpins so much of our lives.

The government told a story about me before I was born. Strangers who took me in were given a story and they too had their own stories.

I never turned up at a stranger's door just to be me; the story always arrived before me.

Throughout a childhood in care, I was morphed into believing I was some kind of monster – just by those stories, let alone others' actions. I believe the discrimination that underpins many of the awful things I was taught to believe about myself as a child has some of the most destructive long-term consequences. For those of us who did not have a positive experience in the care system, deconstructing that damage could easily take a lifetime.

I did not want to deal with my history, publicly or even with friends, so I did therapy and made art, or music, or wrote and carried a burden that impacted my life irrevocably both in my ability to function at all at times, or be part of the world, but I always kept trying, in small ways, to connect myself more strongly to this life.

Twenty years after I put away that manuscript, I once again thought I might die.

As we do at such moments, I turned to God. My God is the primordial matriarch who created all things 13.9 billion years ago out of a huge explosion of energy, all of rage, all of fury, all of creation, all of destruction, all of the atoms and particles and carbon of stars that make up every one of us. I asked her – what could I trade for my life? If I could be allowed to have more time, to see my child grow up and maybe meet their children, what value or purpose could I give back for such a thing? The answer was *Ootlin*.

I had a story that was more politically important than anything else I might write. I did not want to even look at it again but it was calling me.

This is a story I have never told.

It is a story about how some stories saved me and others destroyed me. I am writing this to reclaim myself from all the stories put upon me, that were often little to do with me.

On the day the Freedom of Information Act came in I picked up the phone at 9 a.m. It took me twenty-four years to get my social work files. I collected a vast heavy load of files. Hundreds, thousands of pages, many redacted in black lest they validate something that would allow me to sue the social work department, or those who had raised me, or to protect others' identities, but often to safeguard the system. I had lived in so many placements. I had several name changes. I lived in foster families, had two adoptions, many short- and long-term placements in children's homes and hostels. I had been through more as a child raised by the state than I could ever get my head around. I had never got to have my say about my time in the system, legally or otherwise.

I suffered from severe anxiety and a devastating loss of self that came from lifelong brainwashing telling me that I was the problem. I've never met an abuser who owned what they did, or a system that wanted to be accountable.

Society raises us to avoid any subject that can make us vulnerable or cause shame.

It is no longer my shame to carry.

There are a lot of kids out there being told they are less than everyone else. They are made unsafe by that story alone.

Ootlin is a message of solidarity to any other person who has ever had to overcome, in any small or greater way, the power of someone else's story or legislation or law, which was devised solely to dehumanise them.

We are all of us bound by stories, yet some of us are more negatively impacted than others.

This is a story about a little girl who learned to examine narrative very, very, very carefully and always in secret. This is a story about a girl who found her way to books, and discovered in a world of words the only place she ever actually belonged.

I sought out cultural mothers by the time I was in my teens. Their words, voices, art raised me or at the very least offered solace or company. I spent a lot of time alone both in the system and after it. Some of my favourites included Nina Simone, Alice Oswald, Maya Angelou, Dorothy Allison, Billie Holiday, Frida Kahlo, Tracey Emin, Louise Bourgeois, Patti Smith, Lydia Lunch, Poly Styrene, Odetta, Hole, Sylvia Plath, Anaïs Nin, Nan Goldin, Yayoi Kusama, Nina Cassian, bell hooks, Nawal El Saadawi, Elizabeth Bishop, Blondie, Leonora Carrington and Cookie Mueller. I went to the Buddhist teachings in words and sometimes in person, also to Wiccan practices and origins which had pulled me towards them all my life. I studied all the religions I could find and considered the myths that predated some of them; I sought out science and medical texts and music; I read about philosophies, art movements, and social or psychiatric developments; I did it all while looking to the sky every single day and asking with every atom of my being – why are humans here at all?

No answers that I could find ever really convinced me.

I sought out cultural fathers or brothers in Viktor Frankl, Ice-T, Nick Cave, Kurt Cobain, George Orwell, Knut Hamsun, Reinaldo Arenas, Max Ernst, David Lynch, all the great grunge bands, and post punk and new wave and no wave, Burroughs, Ballard, Basquiat, Hendrix, Public Enemy, Kafka ... I didn't agree with all of them the whole time but I didn't have any family I'd ever met that I could remember and so I turned to culture and asked it to raise me, to teach me, to – in my most isolated moments of which there were many – let me have somewhere to rest, and return, and belong.

Now I must offer back my own lighthouse on a distant shore, for anyone who may need such a thing.

This is my story. It is only my perspective, imperfect as that will of course be. I never claimed myself properly, nor my own history. These are only my memories and they are not told for revenge or 'from rage' or out of bitterness. They are told to honour the great light of being! It is given to us all by the primordial matriarch. I have always felt like the carbon of her stars is strong in me and I am grateful.

Twenty years after I first wrote this memoir I opened that flight case, took out an old yet pristine typed-up manuscript and I revisited it. It is the hardest thing I have ever done in my entire life. I never shared the story, of my childhood, or a decades-old note that turned into a memoir of my own life, with anyone.

Until now.

This is the book you are holding.

PART ONE

Age 0–5

I

I wanted to be pure so badly but before I was born I almost killed my mother. It was not a small overdose. She shook a bottle of tablets, popped it open, forced pills down her throat until it burned and the world began to fade.

At five months pregnant a growing foetus doubles in size.

It was no longer possible to ignore me.

She lit a cigarette.

Waited for one of us to die.

I could hear her heartbeat as it began to slow – down.

The room got darker.

Much later a bright light is shone in her eyes.

Paramedics have to carefully navigate her pregnant body down a small concrete stairwell in a low-rise block of council flats. She is wheeled out past her neighbours, in one of the roughest estates in the country. Doors close. Ambulance indicates right. Turns onto a motorway. There is a hum of the engine and a medic asks, how many? The motorway is all cats-eyes. It goes on and on. A gap appears in the trees and the ambulance turns onto a hidden road that leads to one place only. It drives slowly past the groundskeeper's accommodation; he looks out the window, raises his hand and picks up a stubby pencil to record the arrival in a book. Signs say 'Watch Your Speed'. A small roundabout sits by a car park with industrial buildings in it. A tall row of fir trees shield the view. Patients walk in the grounds. Nurses or sometimes family visitors chaperone them. A long winding drive delivers the ambulance into the middle of a vast psychiatric village. End-less black skies roil across two hundred and twenty-two acres of grounds.

The vehicle slows to a halt in front of a gargantuan arche-typal Victorian asylum building which stares out across the entire site. It presides over thirty villas, each filled with patients with different ailments, mostly alcoholics in Villa 7, abuse survivors in Villa 19; there is a locked ward for women considered too dangerous to be allowed out in a prefab build-ing up on the hill. The lit-up buildings are surrounded by darkness. In the distance, cars race down the motorway like electric eels in the night. A tiny wooden prefab building creaks in the cold wind. It has SHOP painted haphazardly on a sign above it. There is a rehabilitation centre, a workshop, a village hall. There is a laundry, and the nurses' training centre. A huge incinerator on a hill where black smoke trills out day and night. A tall church designed by H. O. Tarbolton and a minister who will not bless me. There has been someone on reception admitting patients here since 1902. It was run by the Edinburgh District Lunacy Board back then. It had a train that ran one way only until a patient decapitated themselves on the line. It stopped after that. Of those patients who committed suicide it often occurred within weeks of arrival. Nearby, nearly eight hundred naked bodies lay stacked on top of each other in unmarked graves. Some kind of resting place for those who appeared to have nobody to claim them. As the administrator took my mother's name (again) (it was not her first time there) I turned in the blood-glow of the womb.

They wrote down a number.

Assigned a bed.

I listened for the lilt of her voice.

Silence!

Instead there were other noises. Tablets rattling on a metal trolley, someone scrunching up a plastic cup; footsteps, echoey corridors; television, canned laughter; a scrape of forks; a flurry of thuds, a door closed hard, the spark of a lighter, two people inhaling, someone said the same word over and over again like a prayer, or a mantra.

Not a sound from her though!

My arms were too short to reach out in the womb.

I was floating in space.

I could stretch.

I could yawn.

I was translucent.

Blood vessels were visible through my skin. There was a cage around my heart made of bone. I was kneeling on the altar of fate!

My heartbeat had its own drum separate to hers, a tiny fast metronome. I had been sent here straight from the other side – some kind of earthly assassin, a fanged one, a fallen angel, a nothing. I was thoughtless and wordless with see-through hands – splayed in front of me.

I had ill intentions.

And, I was so very far from wanted.

Still, I wasn't leaving.

I needed calcium – so I took it.

I weakened her teeth.

I had a fine coating of hair all over my body called lanugo.

I had been the size of an apple pip, then an avocado, then as long as a carrot!

My eyes already had colour in them.

There was shouting out there, something was always going on. The outside world was a frenetic place, I needed more than a wall of placenta between me and it. I wanted to dwell in the quiet bliss of amniotic suspension forever. I was surrounded by two membranes – amnion and chorion. My mother came from a family of Catholics named after saints and she could not terminate easily at all. Stuck with a growing tumour inside her, she had no choice; I weighed about 1.3 pounds on our attempted death day.

I was not meant to be here.

My imprint was more than faint.

I was a sin, an exit, a locked door; I opened a portal to the other side that could not be shut; I came from the underworld but would say nothing of what went on there; I had notions of immortality; I was a parasite, a bastard and a leech. I was a dark room and a dress being tugged down. I was a hangover. I was bad sex while too drunk; I was a broken heart; I was a disappointment. I was a permanent sense of unease – crescendoing towards colours so bright and vicious my mother could not bear them.

I brought the voices.

I was unstoppable.

While she settled into ward life the hospital psychiatric team arranged a meeting to decide what would be done with us. Lots of patients slept heavily sedated, a thick chemical blanket to tuck them in. Some just lay staring. Late at night when the wards were dimly lit, monsters swam around them.

They were my first playthings.

In a corridor, tall metal files stood shiny and steel with uniforms hanging neatly pressed in each one.

Polished black shoes were placed side by side.

Leather restraints sat in drawers.

Shock treatment required a small cushion dipped in water.

There were rows for bottles, all colours of tablets, needles – sharp and sterile. Stores held shelves of antiseptic, plasters, bandages, bleach, nit cream, cheap shampoo, carbolic soap. There were a lot of thin folded towels. Corridors turned to find more corridors, they locked onto each other. Such high ceilings in the big village hall! Ornate cornices! The site also had newer prefab buildings built in the war. They rotted a little more each year in the relentless north wind, not in any way fit to keep out Scottish winters. There was one lift in a building up on the hill that none of the nurses would go in. The monsters had taken over that one a long time ago. I could have gone in it. I'd have sat there as a toddler and played all day – quite happily. Those monsters were the first creatures to love me and I had no reason to discriminate between the dead and the living and only one of those wanted me – so it was those I favoured.

Trees rustled outside.

A crescent moon hung cleanly above the huge old asylum.

The monsters sang me lullabies. They told how some people never left here, or how others sat at windows for decades, and how some fell in love and yet more managed to walk out a little more well than they were before they came in. How some people were so glad of this place as a refuge. How nurses and doctors fulfilled their training here. How there was one doctor who used to bring his little girl into work sometimes and she'd play in the grounds and say hello to all the patients who passed her by. The big hall was always decorated for Christmas festivities. They told me about soldiers who arrived here after both World Wars to roam the grounds in a haze of tobacco and chlorpromazine. In the really old days, patients would carefully write letters to family and give them to staff but they were never sent. Those patients would sit day after day watching for a relative to arrive but none was ever going to come. Those letters were kept in secret, so the doctors could study lunacy.

Each morning my mother sat on our ward.

She wanted to go.

The following week the psychiatrists' scheduled meeting was finally held.

My arrival was discussed with trepidation.

Severe psychosis was likely.

They noted her prior admissions to the hospital, once for three months after the birth of her first child, several other occasions, and one of particular note during extreme and disturbing visions on LSD. Another note of intrigue was raised at the meeting. It was point 3. As the secretary poured hot tea and they selected biscuits from a plate, they agreed that it was curious to find out that my mother's biological mother (who she had not grown up with) had been hospitalised on another psych ward at a different hospital not so long before we had. My paternal grandmother had been having ever more extreme delusions about my mother's pregnancy until she had to be sedated as well. I took out two generations before me with madness and I hadn't even met them to smile. I was an awful thing. All love though! It is all newborns have to give. I wasn't sure either of us would make it. They discussed my mother's prior shock treatment and debated the success and limitations of various recent advancements in medication. They went over the details of her long hospitalisation after the birth of her first child, just five years before. Carrying and delivering a baby had also precipitated that breakdown. They discussed with some frustration that my mother still refused to sign a soul and conscience certificate, and they agreed she was too ill to represent her own truths. She knew a child might grow up and read such a certificate one day and so she wasn't going to do it. The staff wrote things down anyway. They said that her husband (not my father) had told her he was living in a hippy commune but it turned out he was actually serving a sentence in Wandsworth prison for drug offences. He was a registered heroin addict, so they checked files to see if she was too. My biological father was an old boyfriend who they said was rumoured to drink a lot, and who was rarely present, and they concluded he was of no use to anyone, although his influence was important to my mother. It was agreed by all those present that her modes of life rendered her unfit. There was discussion of me being raised by nuns. Or, being handed over to a Catholic adoption agency on the day I was born. One of the newer doctors said he'd heard that one of my great-grandmothers had been the most famous drunk in Glasgow and how much did you have to drink exactly to claim that? How they chortled! Over cups stained with tea and plates covered in crumbs, it was agreed that one way or another I was going to be born. My mother would be hospitalised. I would be taken. It was decided. They put it on file. From that day on the state had set it in motion, it was only a matter of time before they owned me.

2

It was close to midnight when I was born. Leaves fell from trees in reds, golds and ochre. Some of them were see-through with fine skeleton veins that would crumble under even the lightest touch. Or crunchy brown leaves that lay underfoot. Or big tough red leathery ones around tree trunks. Mice began to burrow. It was dark. Stars mapped out roads across the grounds. Bonfires lit by groundsmen smouldered. Everything smelled of damp mulched earth and woodsmoke. An icy wind whistled up through wooden floors until each asylum building was cold as a tomb. It furrowed paths through long grass. The incinerator groaned. Up on the maternity ward I was lifted into the air. Taken to another room to be inspected while my mother was rushed away to begin her treatment.

I was wiped, weighed, tagged, swaddled – taken to the car park and handed over to a person who drove me away. I was out into the world without her on the very first day I was born. I strained to hear her voice, or heartbeat, or laugh, or even the way she cleared her throat. My mother was gone. Sore and swollen and hormonal, she would have been taken back down to the psych ward to begin her treatment.

I was in a car and it was going somewhere.

On my files it does not say where I lived for the first few months of my life.

There is no address.

There is no name.

There is no keeper.

I like to think it was goblins. Cave-dwelling, heavy-drinking, knife-wielding, poetry-spouting, foul-mouthed, chain-smoking – outlawed from the human world and not at all maternal but oddly taken by this strange foundling, goblins!

In lieu of other names they called me ootlin.

One of the queer folk who never belonged, an outsider who did not want to be in.

In reality it was actually the ancestors who were the ones to accompany me out of the hospital. As I was put in a car they argued (as the dead do ceaselessly in eternity) about who had fucked up the family line most and therefore inadvertently caused this predicament. Such brutal fights! Later on that night they sat around my very first crib giving each other dirty looks. They debated whether I would survive what was coming. It was unlikely. The ancestors with their strange faces and eternal habits inspected me. I slept with fists curled tight. I didn't want to open my eyes. I was trying to make my way back to the underworld. I had not left it in the way infants are meant to because there was no mother to pull me into this one and I had already learned on the first day I was born that all things end. I already knew in all my tiny bones there would never be a real home for me on this planet.

I was not meant to be here.

I had been sent by some awful, hideous, mistake.

I drifted.

Files began to pile up in social work offices. They were typed up with multiple variations of spellings of my name(s) (nineteen within the shortest time), a spattering of dates of birth they rotated depending who was on shift. The humans paid to document me had no idea who I was, or my actual age, or what I had actually been named. Still. They had things to write so they did. Back on the ward my monsters swam around at night looking for me. They were sad as I was to be separated. It must have been a relatively rare thing at least, for them to have a little plaything who had delighted so – in all the stories they told.

3

On the ward my mother just had to be a patient for a little while.

A rare respite.

It was a place to breathe.

Somewhere she could be ill in all its totality.

Not have to try and pretend to feel well enough to cope with everything.

A small time away from the council scheme she lived on that was designed as some kind of a social experiment. Her family had gone from the high-rise tenements in Glasgow (which is where she'd met my father – a neighbour – both of them just kids then and living on the same fifth-floor landing) to a newer estate with lots of low-rise council flats in an area where there was mostly just a motorway, and a shopping centre, and a school.

On the ward they measured out her meds.

They wrote notes on her but did they ever ask her what happened?

How her heart got broke?

Meanwhile they made notes about the mental illness that ran in our genetics. The female line mostly. Psychotics, schizophrenia, suicide, severe depressions. They didn't mention the visions of hard smart tough men, like my grandfather, who my father would one day claim had been an old-school gangster but what do I know, I had never met them as a kid that I can remember, just gleaned what I could from social work files which say my father never returned their calls and drank constantly, the few meetings I had with him as an adult were usually in train station bars where he'd be drinking. It's not like I knew any of them anyway so what did it matter really? I was told my grandfather had visions as I do. It's a thing. We were born like this. The files said my mother's family were notorious in their area supposedly and, as was (and often still is) the way of things, they commented on her modes and habits and her sickness rather than her soul. Did they examine the impact of poverty? Or her history? Or the great disease of a society that casts its own people out all the time?

People were released from asylums more in the late seventies. It used to be you went in and never came out.

A general idea of rehabilitation was becoming fashionable.

Recovering in the community was the plan once you became less of a threat to yourself, or others. The shame and fear of being mentally ill would always be on you though. Like a red stain under your fingernails. Madness was thought to be catching. It was considered to show weakness of personality, or even immorality, or possession, or evil? Some thought it was a made-up thing but all agreed it was something to fear.

Anyone could end up like that …

They too could run out of their homes in the dead of night to scream uncontrollably while neighbours bolted their doors and authorities were sent to take them away and lock them up so they would not infect the good people who had not yet succumbed.

At the next meeting a fresh shiny packet of rich tea biscuits was unwrapped and tea was replaced with coffee and little brown creamer pods with sugar for a touch of luxury. Months after my mother's latest admittance to the psychiatric hospital and with loose skin on her belly a little softer than before, the doctors brought a stamp down on my mother's file – she was about to be released.

Little me with a different name, first and last.

4

My brother scuffs his feet since she got us both home to stay with her again and he clenches his fists and inspects her to see if she is really well this time. He bites his nails. Looks over his shoulder. My brother is six years old now and he keeps his hands balled because I broke his mother. It's not like she was fixed before I came so it's not even like I was breaking a whole thing and that's hardly fair.

It is his duty to get rid of me.

School time is the only respite from this.

Door slams.

Breathe!

Often, I just have to go back to bed, where she will sleep, or smoke in the dark.

Light through curtains.

Lay, lay, lay.

Bored, hungry, there is a click of a rosary bead at some point, voices in another room later on; sometimes there is the clink of glasses and music and laughter!

I don't cry much.

Or, as little as possible and I don't hold my hands up expecting to be lifted all the time.

It seems to me like my mother has got a gigantic stone boulder strapped to her back at all times so just making it to the bathroom takes her a gargantuan and overwhelming effort and then she must recover her strength when she sits back down and I hold my breath in case she does not make it next time.

Social worker comes to ask how things are now.

My biological mother explains that the visible rocking and drooling (side effects from the meds) are really embarrassing.

A social worker in an office types up notes all about us and keeps them on file:

Unchanged nappies. No toilet training. Mother sleeps all day. Can't be left alone with brother. Brother a concern at school, he hurts children and shows no remorse. Boy is so neglected he appears retarded. Boy is found wandering on estate at midnight with bruises asking staff from day centre to take him in. Both children have weeping infected sores all over their bodies. Covered in scabies! Record of severe malnutrition. Both children are taken into care again. Then again, and again, and again. Mother back in hospital. Mother leaves hospital too early. It is a pattern. Feels guilty for not looking after the children. The girl has started to wet herself when she sees certain men on the street lately. Girl is also scared of cars. She meets mother in street one day and neither child nor mother recognise each other. Must place brother separately. Not safe to keep them together. Girl found wet from head to toe and no explanation. Girl not quite as fat, trying to stop her eating bad food.

People change like traffic lights.

There is a steady disintegration in my mother's ability to stay alive. I watch. Endless minutes punctuate week-long days. I see every little thing – until they come to take her, again. It is me that is killing her, everyone can see it. Just my presence is enough to cause my own mother's death. I feel it and so does my brother. At night I lie as still as possible right in the middle of my bed. It's not a comfortable way to sleep but I do it in whichever person's house I find myself in. If I go a millimetre right or left, a man under my bed will reach a long arm up to get me.

I won't make it back to my body if he gets me this time.

Can't leave it like that again.

I had to leave my body before. There was a bang and a smell and a certainty that I would die unless I left myself behind instantly. My body does not trust me any more. I betrayed it by leaving it on its own to deal with what I could not.

In the social work files it says that whenever I see a certain kind of man in the street, dark hair, tall, a particular look – I wet myself immediately.

Days turn into nights and one morning I get up and my brother has gone.

They took him.

Soon they will take me.

I won't ever see my brother again.

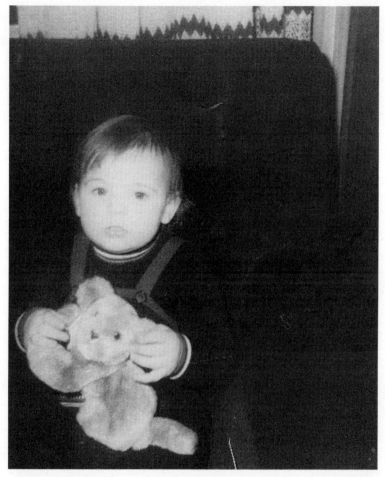

Going to another place to live, that is not mine, my normal way of life.

5

The car windows are tightly closed. A cardboard lemon spins under the mirror. I only want two things in this life. Hair long enough to put it into bunches with bright coloured hairbands and the Incredible Hulk to rip this car roof off and save me. He is my only hero. There is a click-click of an indicator light. Kick tiny brown scuffed shoes against the front seat until the person driving tells me to stop. The world is very fast outside. It runs away from the car. The government take me from place to place. They pay people to keep me. I must be very dangerous. Other children – stay in the same houses forever with people that know them. I don't know what the Incredible Hulk would make of that. I never know the people I go to live with. Each new person opens a door like a bird's wing and I have to go into their nest.

Then they close the door.

That's the worst bit.

Whoever they are then turns to look at me.

I don't get to leave for a while then.

It could be good, or it could be something else.

There are things you learn by moving all the time, like all carpets swallow children, not all televisions sound the same, different rooms change the views. I like to look at the small things. A door handle, or the way a woman greets a man when he comes home, how her shoulders hunch, or rest, and what that might mean about what you hear later on. I always look under the bed. I do it each night. I sing about everything I've done all day too, send my voice on ahead of me into every room. People talk different and they don't all smell the same. They wear things – dressing gowns or jeans, tracksuits, skirts; sometimes I see them get out the bath with skin all shiny and wet. Some people have eyes with nothing behind them. They are nowhere people. I don't ever meet anyone who has my exact eyes. I know because I check everywhere I go, hoping I might see someone who looks just like me one day. Nobody has my exact hair colour and my skin is so pale like a ghost child, see-through with bright blue veins, and dark circles under my eyes.

My shoes are always worn at the heel because I don't know how to walk properly.

So many mothers say it!

Walk properly!

I wasn't taught how to do it. I don't know how to breathe either. It's like there is a manual somewhere everyone else got to read while I just gasp in air like a goldfish dying in a little plastic bag on its way home from the fair. Each of the women in all of the houses that I go to live in is called a mother. It doesn't make them all the same. They aren't often like each other but all of them put on a face for when people are there and then there is another one when the others are gone.

A radio is on low in the car.

There is a stack of paper on the front seat with my numbers on it.

Wherever I am going this time, I will tell them – you can't cut my hair! I will point my finger so they know that I mean it. Strangers meet me and then cut my hair! I want bunches!!!!! It's all I want! Just one thing! I want to be pretty! If I was pretty then someone might want to keep me. They should write it on my notes. DO NOT CUT HER HAIR! Or else! Instead they all just go ahead and cut my hair and I find myself standing like a skinned rat in some strange bathroom with people I've never met before while they tut over the absolute state of me.

The car stops, engine clicks off.

Dizzy.

Breathe in and then out.

There is a house with square-eyed windows and a thin oblong mouth. A woman in the front of the car checks her bag, glances at me, she steps out and I just stare straight ahead. None of this is anything to do with me.

– Come on then, missy, get out.

I always remember the sound of a gate as it creaks opens. Memorise weeds on a path. This garden inclines up so it makes the house seem bigger. What is beautiful? I search for one thing that will be my good thing today. A snowdrop! Look! It is so pretty. Doorbell rings. Ding-dong! Ootlin calling! The social worker checks her watch. Adults do that a lot around me. They have set minutes to escort me before the government stops paying them and then they go home. The social worker smiles. I am the same height as the letter box. I want to put chubby fingers through it and sing to the house – ding-dong, the witch is dead!

There are footsteps. Door opens. A person looks down.

Hello!

– This is her?

– This is she!

They both inspect me. Am I to stay a night? Or a week? I never ask. I had a name that was a song once, but nobody here sings it; it was a tiny little song each time it was said and I miss hearing it. As we go into the house they talk.

– No, just a short-term placement, of course we know, I can't believe you weren't contacted earlier.

I am the most stupid thing in existence.

– Go and play!

In a bedroom I find three girls all older than me. I don't take one more step. Sometimes you know it is best to just stand in a doorway.

– This isn't your house, you do know that?

It's a big girl with a ponytail who sneers as the other two giggle hysterically.

– Aye.

– They aren't your parents and this is my room, these are my toys, and you can't play with us! What age are you?

– Three.

– Look at your scaffy clothes, ya wee tramp, piss off!

I am a thing in a body.

Walk backwards.

Maybe I should travel the world like this?

This house smells of mince and tatties. I spy a tiny bathroom at the back of the hall and sidle along the wall. There is a blue toilet with a Spanish dolly with frilly skirts sitting on a bog roll. She is about as happy as I am to be here. Maybe I'll help her escape then only one of us has to stay. Those girls will be sorry when the Incredible Hulk gets here and rips the stupid doors off. I'd be so fucking happy! I am not allowed to swear. They say there are bad words and good words. There are not. There are only words.

6

His name is Bill. His eyes are kind. He is my new social worker
and I think I like him more than anyone I've ever met. I'd pick
daffodils to put behind his ear. He makes me feel super safe.
Bill doesn't say my name weird. He doesn't mind when I'm
silent. He lets me eat sweets and get this – he is taking me to
the zoo. Who does that? I'm not having to sit in an office or a
car or drive somewhere or go to a house to meet strangers and
live there. Not this afternoon! Bill says I have one job only
today and that is to have fun. I am so grateful I could cry. I get
a ticket to hold! I go through a gate! He takes me to see the
monkeys! I love each and every one of them. I wave. I jump
up and down. I clap my hands. There are birds with all bright
colours in an aviary, and a hippo who yawns big fat pearly
teeth.

When my legs get too tired we sit on a bench and eat ice
cream together just happy like that.

It is the best day of my entire life.

– The next people might want to keep you, he says quietly.

– Really? Sounds weird.

We don't get away with having fun forever but he stole me
from the other stuff for a little while and I won't ever forget it.
In the car I begin to change. I get quiet. I am readying myself
for what might be behind the next door. When I get to a new
house someone will come to the front door and take a look at
me to see if I was what they ordered. Like stuff from the catalogue. Keep! Return! Return! Return! Return! Keep! Some of

them say they might not return this one but they don't know me, so it isn't me they want to keep, it's just – somebody, they want to keep somebody, and what they get is me.

My face is the worst!

It goes into a smile, for anyone, and they can be as mean as they want and I just keep smiling and ask if I could do any-thing else to make them happy. I'd even say thank you. Strangers insist you smile when you go to live in their house because it makes them feel like you won't creep up to them in their sleep.

The mother in this house has a grey cloud.

Sits under it.

All day!

Calls it to her like a dog if it goes too far away.

There is a pebble beach nearby and it is grey too, and the house is grey with tiny gritty stones like spiky baby teeth on the walls outside. The path is concrete and all the other houses are grey, and the sky is usually grey, and the sea is grey or black or dark blue, and people's skin is pretty grey and their minds are grey and we live in this freezing-cold rainy grey country called Scotland. Bill isn't grey. He's sky blue. When I laugh he looks like he just won something. I wish he didn't ever have to leave. He's not going to be my worker for long though. The cloud mother sits me down to show me a book. It tells a story that's meant to be about me. I don't recognise anyone in it. I've no idea what she is talking about. When she is gone I cut up all the photographs.

Pretty pleased with myself!

The foster mother likes me less each hour that passes.

One day she tells me that my real family, my biological mother, grandmother and aunt, are being allowed (by the

social work department) to come and visit and then her tongue
slivers out and eats a fly off the ceiling. She is talking non-
sense. I don't have a real family. She makes me wash my face
and comb my hair and sit with my hands on my knees all day –
so the real family can come and look at me.

– Oh, I can't believe your real family would leave you sitting
all day like this!

When her husband comes home later she talks about it
loudly. How awful are my real family? Who could do that to a
little girl? I don't know what her husband is like or if he
answers or if instead of a face he just has a brick. Can't picture
him. Don't even look at him once. I stay away from men. I
don't like them. Except from Bill. If he ever got in trouble I'd
sort it out for him.

The next morning there is a knock at the door.

I have to sit on the same sofa as the real family come in and
they stand in a row in the living room (three of them, one old,
one less old, one sort of young). They all look at me. One of
them has long dark hair. She has long red nails and trousers
that look like black leather. I have to show the real family my
toys and the grey mother is nervous. It's not quite as good as
the Incredible Hulk visiting (any day now ... I know he's on
the way) but it is something.

As soon as they are gone she calls the government.

– You have to come and get 'it', now!

I am not called by name here now. I am called 'it'. She
strings words together with hot rage. They must send a
car to come get me quick, or else. I look at the door where
my family walked out. Maybe my biological mother is a
robot. They made her in a factory. They sent her out with a
mechanical mind to look for her blood-born child. Maybe we
both have tin hearts. She was very pretty to me. The woman

with long dark hair. I thought she was beautiful. I told her I was three years old now. There are so many houses and flats and stairs and faces and none that I recognise as anything to do with me; the social worker says I've moved over ten times.

Me and the mum with the grey cloud.

7

I put my arm around a big pink teddy who is sat on the sofa beside me.

– Smile for me, come on, do it properly!

I bare my teeth.

Behind me there is a wall of long red curtains.

There is a new social worker and she tells me that because I have been saying things (like I want a forever and ever family) now my dream is going to come true and I just need to go upstairs and say goodbye to the grey mother first and then I can go to the forever family who are already waiting on me.

I drag myself up along the carpeted stairs on my knees as slowly as I possibly can.

– Bye!

I say it to a dark room that doesn't answer.

This house doesn't look quite so scary on the way out.

Get into the car with the woman who is not my social worker (I don't have one any more, this one belongs to the new family and they made Bill go away and I hate it) and she talks about a big house with an orchard and she is so impressed I think she might want them to be her new mummy and daddy. The new family's social worker tells me the forever family have lots of older kids and space and the mother used to be a teacher so she is very good. Very good! Very, very, very good!

Fields.

Green!

Skies race along all wispy today.

My new big teddy bear Pinky is coming to live in the forever family too. We are going together. We sit right next to each other on the back seat. He is almost as big as me. I squeeze him. So he knows he is not alone. When he goes through the next door (his first time – not mine), he won't have to be scared cos he has me.

I loved my teddy bear Pinky the most.

8

I cannot stop my heart. It beats and it beats and it beats and it beats! A forever and ever mum and dad are right behind the next door. I have been told not to say bad words in all the new places but really, holy shit! The new family are going to burst out with confetti like on Saturday-night telly and then someone will jump out and blare car horns and a girl will walk around in a gold bikini and a man in a suit will have a huge smile and then I'll win a helicopter! The audience will all clap as I fly it the fuck out of here.

Still not swearing.

Nobody needs to worry, I just say it in my head ...

I hope they don't notice my hair. It doesn't grow much on my head, it stays short forever (even if everyone does keep cutting it) whereas on my body there is a stripe of fine dark hair down my spine like I am some kind of small warm animal. I never look back. If I do – I know who could be looking at me. I have a memory of a memory. I put it in my pocket. I take it out sometimes. Turn it over and look at it. I get paler. My eyes get darker. I do not sleep. I won't do it here either. I wouldn't sleep in this new house (when they open the door) even if God himself was sat right at the end of my bed, chain-smoking and singing songs and swearing like a bastard and keeping shottie for me.

If I go to sleep, the man will come and I will disappear entirely.

Just like my brother.

9

There is a ceiling. It is very high. It's having nothing much to do with any of us. There is a staircase. There are too many rooms. I make my fingers into a steeple. I can do that. There was a church somewhere. I took the steeple with me. I took the cat's cradle too. It is in my fingers. Sometimes I show it to people when I meet them but only if I like them. I don't like anyone here. It is just me and the mother in the house all day while her older teens and husband go to the outside world. One night they might not come back then I'd be stuck with her. There is an Aga in the garden. I make mud pies in it. It is pretty much the best thing in the whole world to do. I run across fields under white skies. I dig into the mud with stubby little fingers and prise china from the earth, all broken triangles, or little squares with different patterns. Blue and cream. Red and orange, yellow with little ducks on it, or green with pink flowers and cracks all over them that are just so pretty. Rub them clean. Trace my finger around the edges. Smoothed by seasons. I hide them in my pockets. My secret treasure. It belongs to me.

Race over towards the orchard to stamp on rotten apples.

She appears at the door.

A name gets shouted, over and over!

Who is she shouting for?

Begin to slow down.

I forgot.

They stole my name.

They took me – away from me.

The only thing I arrived here with is gone and I have to answer to a new name now.

When I arrived here I was someone.

They didn't like it.

She wanted a Jenny.

I am to be thin and stab-push away the half-moons on my fingertips each morning with a metal nail file before I go to nursery.

The new name gets shouted louder – something laced behind it now.

Turn around to show I do understand, yes.

She goes inside.

Hunch down and grab clumps of grass. In that house there is a dim corridor. A cold stair. I fell down it after getting out the bath and a surgeon in hospital showed me an X-ray of my head and told me my head was very strong. Best thing I've been told about myself so far. Downstairs there is a dresser. Every morning I have to put my toes under it to do sit-ups, then cuticles and there will be no bunches here.

The mother is in the hallway when I trudge reluctantly inside.

– Did you wash your hands?

– Yes.

– Come into the kitchen.

Bad feeling.

I wish someone else would come back but nobody will be home until later because they are all out at school or work and the sun is shining so harshly outside and it seeps under the doors in an ugly silence.

She moves around the kitchen and on all the worktops there are plates of food. Climb up onto the stool. Beneath us there is a cellar full of freezers of frozen meat. There is a cold shower down there too.

– Come on, sit up straight. I've made you a nice surprise.

– I don't want ...

She pushes a plate of food towards me. I've walked into something I can't leave. Heart races. Please no! She smiles at me. Registers the look on my face. I can't get down off this stool or she will do something to me. All the oxygen goes out the room.

– Eat.

– I don't want to.

– Yes, you do, it's all you want to do, so now you get to eat, everything!

Curl my fingers into fists and try not to cry.

I don't like night.

That's when she usually comes to get me with this kind of face on.

When nobody else downstairs can hear it the mother takes me out of bed and drags me down a hallway, to a bathroom, closes the door tight and shouts at me. If I have wet the bed she forces me into a nappy, hurting me when she does it, yanking me around, it stings because I have not been a baby for a long time. Her youngest kid sleeps in the attic with me. This is not night-time though. It is right in the bright harsh glare of day and nobody is coming home for hours. Fields lie flat around the house for miles. She pushes a bowl of marsh-mallows towards me. I chew in silence. Swallow. Repeat. She is so, so, so cold. I can't stop seeing the other plates of food and I am crying. Sickly liquid marshmallow burns as it comes up my throat. She slides a glass mixing bowl in front of me as I retch and my eyes water and I'm hot and dizzy and she smiles and takes the bowl of sick and places it in the fridge.

– You can finish that later.

I don't know if what she is saying is real. I hope with my whole heart that it's not. If I can just want it enough all the bad things will go away. She pushes a plate of something else towards me. I am really, really scared now. Heart jumps. I have done everything right! I stabbed the half-moons out of my fingernails. I did my sit-ups. I have left food on my plate each day just like she told me to do, but there is a problem.

– Can I go, please?

– No!

Tears. Plate. Bowl. Knife. Scrape. Tap runs. I watch her. At the bunker opposite she picks up a tin of dog food. Can opener. Metal teeth bite in a circle. Lid pops off. She forks lumps of jellied meat onto a plate. Heart rat-a-tat and clack-clack. Throat closes. So many fires in my stomach. Ice too. Skin so, so, so cold.

– I'm not eating that. It's the dog's food!

She slides the plate in front of me and stares down into me. Hot tears.

Closed fists, tiny and red-knuckled, do not cry, I am not doing it!

She slams the cupboard doors.

– Fine!

Don't look at the plate of dog food. Look straight ahead only. She is so angry! The fridge door is yanked open. A flash of bright light. She slams it shut so hard it rattles. The bowl of sick, congealed and pink, is smacked down in front of me.

A clink as she opens the cutlery drawer and turns around and holds up a cold metal spoon for me to take from her outstretched hand with its horrible knuckles. I am shrinking. Somewhere I can hear a high-pitched sound. My heart is going so fast and I am no longer breathing except for short little gasps and all the air is gone from the room. She stares right at me, and pushes the mixing bowl closer towards me.

– Okay, you'll have to eat this instead then.

I am made of skin and bone and blood and eyes that plead as desperation rises to a high single note that gets louder and louder and louder and louder.

I die.

A spoon is forced into my hand.

10

The social worker comes and the mother and her talk happy and excited and giddy like best friends; I don't really know much about that, I've not made any friends yet so far since being alive. The mother made me dress up as a nurse today. She took a photograph. I had to smile. Yesterday I had my ballet class in the town hall. Leotard, black with a little belt, pink shoes, smell of talc, keep my back really straight, chin out, point fingers just right, stretch arms up. Cup your hands! Bend forward slightly, leg behind you, point other toe towards the bar, look up to the window, move foot so it is in a T-shape with the other one and then rest both hands in front as if holding an imaginary ball, throw it up in the air and then leap in a row, girls thud one after another – right across dusty floors. They measured me for my tutu. I am thinner. The social worker goes away after a while. I didn't even notice if she said bye. She always looks so pleased with herself. Even later on the mother's grown-up kids come back and it is better then and the dog barks and then night marches over the fields and all that stops. The house is dark again – someone rubbed out the day.

Just before my voice went away.

II

Every night it happens lately. There is a silhouette at the bedroom door. I wait for it with dread. I am dragged down a
hallway in the dark. The bathroom door is flung open in
a silent shaking rage. I squeeze my fists tight. Close my eyes.
Clamp my mouth closed. I will not do what she wants. I don't
care if I die. I am turning myself to stone. I will not do one
thing she tells me to do. I do not care if she kills me. I will not
help her in these moments. What she is doing is more than
wrong. I don't know how much time passes. The whole world
is gone. It has left me. It won't come for me, not now, not ever.
I don't care what she says or does. I hate with the purity of
a child. All I want to do is disappear entirely and then she
would not be able to get me. I am learning how to leave my
body.

At some point we walk back down the hallway, I climb into
bed in a haze.

So hurt, so weary.

I wait for as long as I can just hoping she has disappeared. I
finally get the courage to whisper to her kid on the other side
of the room ...

– Why do you let her take me?

There is no answer.

All the way across on the other side of the room there is
only silence.

Wind rattles the eaves, I hear a bird call out there long and
low and eerie, and all around is dark, dark fields and me

beginning to shrink, my heart racing, my skin cold, every muscle locked together so I don't think I can even move.

Look up.

She is still at the door.

Listening.

12

In the cold basement! Shower. Why? Freezing! No towel, where is it? Run. Race up stairs. Naked and wet and have to go as fast as I can past nearly adult boys with my embarrassing chubby little-girl body on show, not to the attic, I don't get to sleep in the same room as her kid any more, keep running, I am not stopping! Room. That is where I go now. It's very small, like a box. Thin bed. Scratchy! Lie down. Don't need to be told any more. Light from the hallway is going. The door shuts in silence. Total darkness. No windows, or doors, or floor, or ceiling. Shrink. Shrink. Shrink. My tongue begins to get bigger and bigger and my body smaller and smaller and smaller and I have had this feeling every single time I ever lay down to sleep but now I go into a sealed black space at night. Soon my body will disappear entirely and the whole world will be this horrifying sensation in my mouth as I – shrink to a tiny, tiny, tiny dot.

Floating in space means you have to let go of everything, even your body.

Every night I go out there.

I am looking through the universe, in between meteors and falling stars and space dust, I am searching for angels, or my real home, somewhere far beyond the curvature of the earth. I never remember what happens after I have shrunk until I am even smaller than a dot because I am gone then, space travelling.

13

My voice is on the end of a kite. There is a long silver string trailing behind it. It is high up in the sky where nobody can reach it. I don't talk any more.

My voice is gone.

For the last few days I've come downstairs to sit on a chair in silence. I do not move until night-time. Then I go back upstairs. I am in the dark all night. Then she opens the door in the morning. I go and sit in the exact same place. I do not move. I do not speak. I don't play. I don't laugh. I do not shine. I saw myself in a mirror. I didn't like to meet my own eyes. I stare strangely back at myself now.

The doctor has come out this morning to take a look at me.

– She's not been to the toilet for fourteen days?

There is a cold stethoscope. Stick my tongue out. He flashes a light in my eyes. I keep my arms straight. Legs dangle down. I kick them slightly because I am still way too little for them to reach the ground.

– Has anything changed in her routine?

– No.

– This is the second time she has done this in a few months, I don't know quite what would be causing it, he says.

He sits back and looks at me.

– Well, it's just maybe that Jenny eats far too much, she says.

The doctor puts his stethoscope in his bag and gets into his car and leaves me here with her.

Some tablets sit in a box and they will force me to go to the toilet soon.

Go back to sit on the same chair all day without moving.

I do it the next day too.

My voice really is almost totally gone now. It's getting harder to make it come back. I open my mouth and silence pours out. My silence is so loud it shakes the foundations of the house. A tiny grain of sand rolls away from stone. Then another, and nobody else knows. They begin to get nervous around me. My silence keeps getting louder. It can't be ignored. It is a roar!

One day soon after this, I am taken to a building and walked down a hallway and shown into a room that looks like a fake kids' play space. I am to be observed in this room, by psychologists. They are going to prove there is something wrong with me and I must be returned as faulty.

– It's so sad she just won't bond with us no matter how much we try to love her!

Four adults look towards me.

On the notes they write that *I am a child who just … can't show love.* The files state it was also suggested the family might need to change, not me.

Back at the house their social worker arrives.

– Where do you want to live, Jenny?

– I'll be fine when I live on my own.

– You can't do that, silly! Where would you like to go?

Look at her. I know they won't take me anywhere I want to go. I draw them a picture of where they are going to take me instead. The social worker picks it up. A small rectangle box. Two windows drawn in brightly coloured crayon. In front of them there are two small trees. A man and woman with lots of curly hair and glasses. They look like brother and sister. I stand in between them – the odd one.

– This current family are a bit like tomato soup, Jenny, and you are ice cream.

– Uh-huh.

– Both are nice but they don't go together.

The social worker lifts me onto her knee then.

It's the worst bit.

She has started doing this because I don't let anyone touch me any more. She has been trying out things like – making me sit on her knee while she holds me, and I have worked out that the quicker I grow still, the sooner I get to climb down.

I am never going to get a tutu.

14

It turns out that I was not the first little girl this mother got. She tried out two different ones before me! One that they got from a friend for a while, and then another one through the social work department. The mother said the exact same things about them that she said about me.

They were greedy.

Enormous!

It was repulsive!

So strange those two little girls both had so many issues just like the ones she says I have.

The mother said one of the little girls was a real flirt too.

One of her boys told me. The social worker knew all about those other little girls before I even came here. It's in the files. I don't say anything when her boy tells me secrets. He is lovely. The only person I like here. They applied to a few places to adopt and had no said to them for years, before getting me through their social worker. My adoption has just been authorised in paperwork and now I am leaving here with a different name, and eyes that don't look like they did before.

I sit in silence until the social worker comes to get me.

At some point I stopped sleeping.

15

I was in a new place for a while. It had a garden. There were two boys. They dressed me up as a clown. Painted a big red smile on my mouth. Drew black flower shapes around my eyes. Blue circles on my cheeks. They painted their faces. We were savages. Stalking each other with a garden hose. Gnashing our clown faces at passers-by. It was too hot. They had a paddling pool! After a few weeks there was another place and one more after that but now I am in the best home on earth. It is a tiny two-bedroom in a block of six council flats. It overlooks a roundabout where cars whizz by all day long. On the other side of the roundabout there is a track where horses race sometimes and the woman who lives in this home is – a mum kind of a mum.

She is the loveliest person.

I smile at her a lot. Don't bare my teeth though. I smile cos I want her to be happy like she makes me feel. She is the best person alive to me. There is a husband. We see him lots! He laughs and makes jokes and I think he is very funny! He is so nice. He has a huge mass of bright ginger hair that grows out in all different ways from his head at once. They are both so honest (they keep fighting because they are getting a divorce but when they do they always ask me to leave the room so I don't have to see blood and guts running down the walls and that's when I go to my room and wait) and they make everything a game and nothing is scary here. Stick my head around the living-room door ...

– Are they gone yet?

It's either a yes, or a no.

Blood and guts can take a long while to drain from a living room.

What I really like is that they tell me each time it is going to happen. I trust them completely because they don't lie to me about anything and they let me know what is coming even if it isn't that good. There are no hidden rooms in this home either. I checked. None! It is just us in a few rooms and I am so relieved by all of it that I get really sick.

A fever so high I can't shift it.

– You have whooping cough, sweetheart.

– What?

– You know that noise you're making when you cough all the time, that whooping? It's a bad cough and you had it when you were a baby, and a toddler.

This is not good.

Finally I found people I really love and now I'm going to die.

She makes me a bed on the sofa so she can watch me the whole time.

This is the best place I have ever been. There isn't one fancy hotel anywhere that could top it. I wouldn't trade this mummy for anything. She brings me fizzy juice called Lucozade which is basically magic medicine. I get glasses of sweet orange-coloured juice with tiny bubbles. All the time she watches over me to see that I'm okay. I feel like the most important kid that ever lived. I tell her I think she is the prettiest loveliest mummy anywhere.

– Can I stay here forever, please?

– Aw, Jenny.

– Pleaaaaaaseee!!!!

I ask it too much. At least three times before breakfast. I stand close so I can hug her leg. She has never called me a bad name or anything. I just know – I don't need to worry about her. She will never take me out of a bed. She is so kind in her soul. Everyone should have a mum kind of mum. Her own mum comes to visit us one day and she is one hundred years old! How amazing is that! I never met a hundred-year-old human before. Impressed doesn't even cover it. The granny is to stay over and she has to sleep in with me. It's very bad. She says it will be fine and we cuddle in but all through the night I grind my teeth. I talk. I sit up. Eyes closed. My arms reach out to fight things. Fists held tight. I kick. I kick and kick and kick – until my one-hundred-year-old granny ends up on the floor. I am a bad human. She just laughs about it. I feel so good here. I have friends too. We play in the stairwell. All the kids are nice to me. They are going to come to my party. I am careful when I go out onto the flat's wee concrete balcony just like the dad taught me to be. One of my friends takes a pee out there one day and we don't tell the adults. It's best not to mention things like that. I get up one morning and bounce through to the living room and the social worker is sitting there.

– You look so much better, Jenny.

I can tell the mum kind of mum is ready to come over and swoop me up.

– Say hello, Jenny.

– Hi.

– Hi! Well, I've come because I've got some very strange information for you, she says.

– What?

– I found you the *exact* house and family that you drew – remember, you said it was where you were going to go and live?

The social worker glances over at the mum kind of mum and then back at me.

– Aye.

My heart drops. My brilliant lovely foster mum can't look at me because she is trying not to cry. I don't want her to feel bad, and I am used to this, maybe she's not, so I go and pat her back like she did when I was poorly.

– Where?

– Not too far from here, and it really is so – well – unusual, because when I saw (she pushes my drawing over to me) – where they live, it is not a house, it's a mobile home, so it looks a bit like a rectangle box and it's in a caravan park and they have two fir trees in their garden in front of the windows and they both have curly hair and glasses – and it is basically exactly what you drew, with you in the middle ...

She taps on the drawing with her finger.

The mum and the social worker both look at each other strangely.

– When do I go?

– Soon.

– Will I like them?

– You will, they're really nice, they don't have any children of their own, and the mother even used to work with disabled kids and she worked in a nursery, so she really does have a lot of experience with children!

– I want to stay here.

– You know you can't, Jenny, this is only a short-term place-ment. Remember, I told you that sometimes there is a forever and ever mummy and daddy and then sometimes there is just ...

I stare at her. She trails off. Picks up her car keys. I stand at the door to make sure she doesn't come back in and upset us again today.

– Are you coming out to play?

It's one of my friends from the stair with long blonde straight hair.

– No.

– Why not?

– Dunno.

The social worker opens the stairwell door below us and it slams shut in the wind.

16

Bright eyes, matching glasses, he is sat on the other side of her, up against the wall. Her smile is held up by hooks. My lovely mum kind of mum cannot stand the new mother. The new parents have come to collect me after my fifth birthday party. My mum kind of mum told the social worker straight that I should not live with this family. Our little flat is full of my friends. We are sugar-high, brittle and angry because after this I have to leave forever. My friends all know I will not get to come back here again and we are all mad about it. The government don't let kids like me go back. Not even to visit. Not even if we want to. I am wearing a long blue polyester pinafore dress with a tartan neck and long lapels. My hundred-year-old granny didn't come because she already said goodbye and I will miss her and I won't even see if she gets to be a hundred and one!

Out on the tiny balcony with my friends we debate different ways to steal me. Someone wees in the corner (again) and we don't tell the adults (again) and they shout at us to all come back in and there is a birthday cake and candles and everyone sings 'Happy Birthday' to me and I blow it out with a heat on my face that is way stronger than the flames on tiny candles because nobody has ever made me feel more loved than everyone in this room right here.

I try not to glance at the new parents.

They have shoes and all the stuff! Knuckles. Soft skin. They wear clothes and they have hair and things.

The new mum purses her lips thinly when I eat my piece of birthday cake.

I am five years old, not really today, but soon.

This flat will not be here in a few hours.

The stair will be gone too.

My bedroom will not exist, it will just fold up and disappear.

A hanging toy with long metal spiral legs that goes boing, boing, boing will disintegrate like it was never here at all. So will the mum kind of a mum and the lovely dad and their blood and guts and their plants and pictures and telly and the sofa where I got well. All gone forever! I will never see them again as long as I live. It hurts so badly! I am going to lose everyone I love and all my friends at once and my whole life has been a series of entire streets and houses and people and accents and skies and rooms disappearing over and over and over and over and over and over again. I didn't even do anything wrong this time. As I wander through the party my friends get louder and the new parents' backs get straighter and there are flashes of me in other places, arriving, leaving, cars, a room without windows or doors, worse things – memories seep into my party under the door like a dark stain.

Hug my friend so hard and she won't let me go either – her sticky arms are strong right around me.

All the kids shout louder and dance wilder.

We force the silence back for one more hour until I leave.

I don't need to ask again why she can't keep me, I know that they are splitting up and they probably wouldn't even give me to just one parent anyway. It is making her sad, so I make an extra effort to jump around and be happy even if I feel so upset … because the mum kind of mum has given me a pure love and she didn't want anything back for it, and I want her to know that even when I go far away from here and never see her again, I will carry some of that light inside me.

The files say things about the new family. Like how she uses me as a scapegoat for her anger already, and that she said she wasn't sure she could ever love me, or maybe anyone, and how she is only taking me because she won't be beaten by a child. It says how her husband says he will always be on her side. So there is them and then, me. It says that she hit me way too hard one time and that she has a lot of concerns about me being a thief. That she finds my greed repulsive. It says the social workers think she is jealous of me and doesn't talk about me in a nice way. It says they have not got high hopes that an adopted child would be intelligent. It says they won't be able to tolerate a thief. It says that several times. It says how she likes silence when eating her lunch, or reading, and she has told them I will just have to learn how to be quiet. The social worker from the last family pushes hard for me to be there. She tells them I need someone strict. She tells the adopted mother to play a game where I am to act like the mother from the last adoption and that when we do it I get incredibly upset.

PART TWO

Age 5–12

17

Caravans dot their way across the park until they meet farmland. Our mobile home is bigger than most; there is a red
concrete porch and I like to get an old bedsheet and place
stones to make myself a little tent in the garden. Most of the
caravans are long, skinny and metal. Some are painted. The
older ones are really faded from snow and rain and hail. They
rest on haunches or bricks and have three wee stairs that go
up to their front door, there are gnomes in gardens, one caravan flies an American flag, another has pretty plants in between
rocks and lots of flowers. The woman there gives people fresh
strawberries. A lot of people grow rhubarb like some kind of
alien fruit on huge thick stalks. Kids snap it off and get a bowl
of sugar and dip the rhubarb into it, then eat it. Some caravans
have broken toys or a bust sofa in their garden, and some have
fences around them but others sit on open ground so you can
just walk right up to them. There is a shop that sells bread and
soup and it smells of tins and dust or, on rolls day, fresh bread.
It has a penny-mixture section and you can buy twenty half-
penny sweeties for 10p! An ice-cream van sells cigarettes with
two single matches for 5p. The adults don't seem to have a
clue what the kids all know and talk about to each other.
Mobile homes are twice as big as single caravans. The bigger
units are driven onto the site in two lorries. They go down
motorways with their living rooms and kitchens and bathrooms just all on show so before you end up living in it your
home is inspected by lots of strangers in cars. Some people are

living in the caravan park for unusual reasons but most people are just really nice. You can't be weak here among the other kids, though, or frightened. There is a caravan away up at the back of the park with dirty lace curtains and Broomstick lives there with fifty-six cats. The kids are scared of her. There is the ice-cream-van man, and the ambulance man, the lesbian schoolteachers, the computer guy, the site guy, the deaf girl who is funny and babysits me and who is teaching me how to do sign language, there's a woman with huge tits who wears a sort of school uniform and long socks and all the mums hate her and all the husbands like her. Through the caravan park next door and out a back lane and across a field and then over a back road where cars go quite fast – there is the big city dump. I am not allowed to play in there. None of us are. It's dangerous. So, we go all the time. There are diggers at the dump with yellow lights spinning on the top. When they see us sneak in there alarms go and they call out over big speakers for us to get out of there.

I am in my bedroom combing my hair which is to stay short because I can't be trusted to look after it if it was long. In her bedroom next door the adopted mum has more dolls than I have ever seen in my life. They all stand with super-straight backs and perfect hair and smiles and porcelain skin and they never get angry and I am not allowed to do that either. If I do I am to go to my room and come back when I've put a smile on my face. The adopted mum is angry every day. She is always ready to explode. I am lucky to be here though. I have a family. Nobody wants older children so I was lucky they took me. They told me so. What would have happened to me if they did not take me? I met the new granny and it was embarrassing as I had to say hello and I'm just a stranger but I liked her so much right away. And the adopted mum's folks too. Her parents are really nice but a bit more official, they have dogs and love the Queen. I only get hit to teach me a lesson. Children need to be hit when they do something wrong. It is how they learn. She has told me that. It's not a punch really. It's a hard slap. Or smacks on the legs. Or the time she slapped me across the face. Or one time she was hitting me so hard I could tell even she was shocked by it. It happens when it is just her and me. Or my mouth washed out with loads of Fairy Liquid because I said damn, my cheeks grabbed and my head shoved under the sink while she pours Fairy Liquid into my mouth and then I have to gulp and spit water and still taste soap all day and that really makes me cry. I mustn't be upset in front of her. She does not want to see a child with a torn face. She tells me to count myself lucky. Children used to be seen and not heard. To be honest, the things that hurt most are the words she says. How I am lazy and greedy and manipulative and I don't deserve friends because I don't know how to treat people, and how I am a little thief and will go to prison when I'm older if I keep stealing and maybe I just stole a biscuit but next time it might be a 10p piece and before I know it I will be banged up for life. She said she was disgusted by my greed. It was only a biscuit! She was seething. I want to learn to read and write and ride my bike and I want to have friends. I am clearly awful or why would everything have been like this for me? I must learn to get everything right. Then she will like me. I am so scared if I don't she might send me back to the last adopted family to sleep in the room that was like a box and sit beside that mother who did all those things to me.

18

Our kitchen table is hard against a wall. The kitchen is a galley one the dad built himself. The wallpaper has names in Latin (I think) for each little bunch of flowers. When I have breakfast I am next to the fridge-freezer and I try to memorise the names of the flowers and I count how many are in each bunch and then each row and the whole grid they make across the wall. The mother drinks coffee and smokes a cigarette for breakfast. I am so hungry all the time. She explains to me that just because you are hungry does not mean you need to eat. I get one Weetabix with a tiny sprinkle of sugar for breakfast each morning. One piece of brown bread with peanut butter for lunch and water from the fountain. A small 'child's' portion of dinner. One rich tea biscuit and a glass of milk before bed. Sometimes I might get a penny mixture or pudding but not all the time. I am on a strict diet. She says I am fat and greedy. I am very lucky they have taken me. I put my bowl in the sink and smile at her and I know that she is glad to see the back of me for the day and I want out of here too. I go out the front door with relief. Count the steps from our front door to the bus stop. If the steps don't add up to the exact same as yesterday, I will go back and do it again. I count everything now. The flowers on the kitchen wallpaper. Foam tiles in the classrooms. I do not step on the cracks or someone will die and it will be my fault. I have learned how to walk while avoiding every crack in a way that nobody notices. I really have to concentrate.

The other caravan-park kids are at the bus stop waiting on the minibus that takes us to school and it's important to try and not let them see that they all terrify me. Yesterday the two older boys that always batter me at break time, they smacked my head off the school-bus floor and I had blood all over my face and I just sat staring out the window not crying. My adopted mum was so mad at them when I got home and that felt nice. It's up to me to learn to deal with bullies though. That's what the adults say. So, the boys just keep kicking fuck out of me.

– Nice duffel coat, fatty!

– Thanks.

– We dinnae really mean it's nice, ya fuckin' retard, ye look like one ay those hundreds of dolls your mum collects!

The bus arrives.

Count the steps and smile at the driver.

Kick to the back of my legs.

The boys push past me sneering and sit up the back and I sit in the middle where they can throw things at me. They will get me on a platform at lunch hour just like every other day – so everyone in Primary 1 to 3 can stand in a circle and watch while they punch me. Not everyone watches but I'd say at least a quarter of the playground does, while they eat their snacks. It is as regular as warm milk and cheese at break time or the men from the coal mine walking up by our school each day in their overalls cos they are going up to the chippy for lunch. People like things that stay the same.

One day I will stop them but not yet because I am too scared.

– Are you adopted, Jenny? You are, aren't you?

I've been taught not to ever talk about that.

We drive past the big coal mine. All the miners are on the pavement lately, they are drinking from flasks and smoking and waiting on a man called Arthur Scargill who is coming from the trade unions to talk because Margaret Thatcher is going to close all the pits down.

– Did you just gob in her hair?

– Noh!

– Did!

– Ah fucking didnae!

– What's your budgie called, Jenny?

– Jodi.

– Everyone's budgie is called Jodi.

– Some are called Joey.

– Are you being smart? Yer mum has lots a pets, ay, bet she likes them more than you, she cannae fucking stand you.

I can't disagree with him. I don't say she lobs her lighter at the budgie's cage when she wants him to shut up cos she's watching telly at night, or that our cats are stalking the cage for fun and it's only a matter of time before Jodi joins the pet cemetery at the back of our garden.

– How come you dress like a baby?

– Noh, I dinnae.

– Aye, you do, my ma heard yours say you're never going to get your ears pierced or even wear make-up when yer eighteen and you'll be in long socks and T-bar shoes forever. She dresses you like one of her freaky fucking dolls!

The school bus pulls to a halt. All the local kids look when we pile out.

Cos we are caravan-park kids.

I get called Gypsy Jenny and they sing the wee song from the advert.

Everyone floods down a sloping playground towards the back doors – one has BOYS engraved in stone above its entrance, GIRLS on the other. We jostle in past a little nook where the dinner ladies are smoking. Our school smells of disinfectant and dust and custard and the laddies' bogs reek of piss. Boys stink. We go through the assembly hall which is also the dining room to get to our classrooms. I do my lessons in a big open-plan Primary 1 and 2 classroom. Someone does a purple shit in the communal toilets. Everyone goes to look. One girl shags the wall to show us how grown-ups do it. At morning break time there is a small bottle of warm milk for everyone and a cube of cheese with a thin warm sheen of grease on it. The story area has a circular rug where we all sit cross-legged. I am always too scared to ask to go to the toilet. I have to really psych myself up to raise my hand. Another kid just pisses himself right there on the rug. Everyone laughs, except from me. I give him a wee pat on the arm when he sits back down with red cheeks. It's not his fault he pished himself.

19

I go over the big letters, then the little ones. I join them up exactly the same size. The blackboard has today's word on it. I have written it down already; I want more. I have been practising writing so much that my finger has a bump on it that never goes away.

I am growing a writing bone.

When I walk into my fairy-tale books I really look at the words – what are they saying? If you don't help the woman by the well then toads will fall from your mouth. I think that's right. I'd help her cross the bridge with her bunions and I'd make sure she was okay and say something nice to her and I wouldn't be doing it so pearls would fall from my mouth, I'd do it because being good starts with small things. I will never be like the people that did bad things to me. I'd rather die. I know exactly why you don't break other humans. Or hurt them. It is the most awful thing of all to do. I know there is something bad in me too or why would so many horrid things happen to me? I chase memories away at night when I go to sleep. I get flashes of things when I'm in class. Sometimes I stick my fists in my eyes until all I can see are stars. I bite my thumb so hard. There is a circle of teeth marks on my skin at least once every day. I'm scared I'll bite my finger off one time. It is better I hurt myself than get angry. The mum does not allow that. She is always angry though. I am just to take it and smile. I am breaking. I read fairy tales like they are the rules of life. I read every other book I can find too. Stories become real things.

They can change our life entirely. I don't tell anyone that the other worlds are real. They are though. I see things in people they don't want anyone to see and sometimes it makes them really not like me. People sense something off me. It's an energy. It's an invisible thing. It makes them not trust me. It is a light I can't get out of me. It makes me gleam. Nobody likes a shining thing. It was my real birthday on the day I arrived at primary school. I sang a sad song all afternoon. The teacher told me I couldn't cry because it was my birthday and without missing a beat I sang to her – a song about a girl at a party who cries if she wants to! I felt a bit better after that. I spent the rest of the afternoon daubing blue and yellow paint on a pinned-up piece of paper. I wondered if my real mother thought about me. It is the only day of the entire year I will let myself think about her or my real family.

I know far better than to tell anybody.

It's my secret.

20

Running at full pelt across the farm field then climbing up onto the top of a hay bale. I feel strong and invincible and like the sky is blue because it loves me. When I get home I am going to read a book under my covers by glow-worm. The library van stops outside our caravan once a week. It is loaning me everything it has to read and the librarian is always so nice to me. I have found a way to escape my world every night.

It is everything!

Words are actual magic.

They take me away to the only place I belong without apology.

21

We are all sitting in our living room staring at the television. All over the country people are doing this exact thing. Watching the same four channels. Our TV has a wooden frame and big square buttons to change channel. My adopted dad takes a drag on his cigarette and gives me a wee smile. My adopted mother sits in her chair. She is closest to the fire. She takes a drag on her cigarette and then her knitting needles start clicking again. I keep getting knitted jumpers from her or the aunties. They are nice. Look much better than jumble sale things. Our wood burner is radiating heat tonight. It is like a giant silver soup pot with a lid on top. They use tongs to take the lid off and drop more wood into it. Every day I think about putting my hand on the stove so my skin melts off.

I think horrid things.

It's winter now so she's not watching telly naked at least.

I hate it when she does that. *EastEnders* is on. She doesn't like to get interrupted when watching telly/reading/having lunch/cooking/walking through a room, or doing anything really. She says she wants them to bring back capital punishment. She's angry that children no longer get the belt at school. She says it is wrong that kids can't even be punished properly by teachers any more. One of her favourite people is Margaret Thatcher, though everyone else hates her. Today we got yum yums at lunchtime and she was not mad at me. Whenever it seems better I begin to hope it will be okay. I am lucky to have a family at all. I love going to see my granny and watching

Columbo with her or having pick and mix from Woolworths or decorating the Christmas cake. Then there are her parents who grow their own veg and make fresh meals and cousins we see once a month and all things in life are never awful. Sometimes I get so excited about being alive because one day I will do something great. I won't always be a scaff. Or like this. I just need to get better at being me and then she will stop flaying my skin off with words (or worse) each day. I am wearing furry all-in-one pyjamas because it is so cold. The heater in the back of our caravan is a Calor Gas one that hisses and smells of gas and glows orange in our tiny hallway all night. Her dolls stand straight at all times. Eyes stare at me when I walk by her room to go to the loo. Pristine and ever-smiling with their little plastic unbrushed teeth! They don't shit. They don't swear. They won't grow up to be murderers. They don't have crazy real mothers. Insanity is not lurking in them like it is in me. There are teddies all over her bed. Then more placed above it. The more you look at all those dolls and teddies – the more appear. She always wants a new one. This mother is a doll collector. I am to be a little old-fashioned dowdy doll with a very shit haircut. She puts me in a pale blue frilly pleated neck blouse, or pink. I hate that more than anything. There's nothing good about being a girl. More and more dolls appear as the year goes on. One day she will have thousands of them. She will sleep in here for the rest of her life surrounded by dolls. She will wake every day thinking of how much she hates me.

I hate myself for it but I still just want her to be pleased with me.

If I do everything right …

It's possible.

I did a thing in secret today. Not that thing that I'm so ashamed about doing every night. Not sneaking a look at his porn mags, or standing in the local shop wondering if I've got the guts to steal a packet of biscuits, and not me wishing the perfect girl with the ski-slope nose at school would get Aids or even just spots all over her face, and not listening to the big kids talk about who has kissed who and showed their tits or got fingered and not pretending that I don't know any of those things and acting like the little Victorian child she clearly grew up thinking she would have one day. Those are not what I did in secret today …

I got a little white notebook with a plastic cover and I wrote a poem in it of my own.

Then another one …

Later I went back and held my breath.

When I opened it – my voice was still on the page …

Not at the end of a kite!

It wasn't vanished from my throat.

I did not have to hold my breath and worry that what-ever I said would be shot down with a long row of deadly arrows.

My voice was on that page.

Not a story told by someone else …

Just my thoughts – I had never seen them before.

I don't think I knew what I thought even once, until I saw that poem.

It came out of me!

Writing is alchemical, like moving things solely with mind control.

Go by the dolls and don't even give them the satisfaction of looking at those judgemental little cunts.

There's a wart on my thumb.

Just in between the soft creased flesh where it bends when I write.

She says it doesn't matter.

It does though.

When they go to make coffee and tea and talk to some neighbour outside and take a break before their next programme, I jab a needle into the wart (I've been doing it for days) and I keep spiking it around rubbing off the blood and doing it again until this time I finally manage to stab into the root and lever it up (it's kept rising like a flesh volcano then falling back in but I've got it this time) and pull out the head of the wart and entire root too.

Toilet tissue.

Blood.

Press on it, hide the bloody tissue in my fist.

They sit back down to watch whatever is next on telly.

22

Ski-slope princess girl will not stop eyeing up my body. I am eight but I need a bra already. I have hair growing on my body that's not just the gremlin stripe down my back. My adopted mum got me to stand starfish in the bath so she could see and I wanted to die it was so horrible. I've still got my shorts for gym on and I'm reaching for my school shirt when Princess stands up with henchmen either side of her (every other girl in our class who doesn't want to be picked on). The entire changing room catches the vibe before a word is gobbed onto the floor.

– Still fat then, Jenny?

– What?

– It's your face though really, Jenny, isn't it, you're ugly, that's why you are – ADOPTED, isn't it …?

She sticks her chin out and puts one hand on her skinny gymnast frame that has never even touched a second-hand bit of clothing …

– What did you say?

– I said no wonder you're adopted, Jenny, who'd want a kid with a face like yours?!

The entire changing room is as silent as the dead.

I never talk about being adopted.

When I look over at her I catch something in her face as she examines my reaction; it's the first time I've ever seen her look confused. Rub tears off my face and get dressed and go along to music class. Everyone is talking about what Princess said to

me, even the boys cos it got spread around. I love music. It is
everything to me. I love words, drawing, and reading as well,
and my best friend at the caravan park who I hang out with at
the weekend, when we are just sitting around telling stories,
or watching movies, or making crazy snacks with random
ingredients, in those moments I feel like I belong somewhere.
Like I'm funny! I think it's what having a family is meant to
feel like. I would never let anyone talk to my best friend the
way Princess did this morning. I love going to see my granny
too. I have good things. My adopted parents have been busy
lately so I let myself in after school and it's less stressful cos I
clean the kitchen and do chores until she gets home. There is
an atmosphere in the music room so electric the teacher with
parrot earrings looks at us all. Princess sits directly opposite
me. A circle of kids in between us. Pure uncut hostility burns
a hole in the carpet. I wish I could tip Princess into it because
she has crossed a line that can't be made okay.

– What's going on then, class?

– Nothing, Miss!

– That's not the case, someone better tell me what is going
on right now.

The whole class falls silent and everyone is looking between
me and Princess.

– Why don't you ask Jenny, Miss?

– Jenny?

– I've fallen out with Princess, Miss.

– Why?

– Because she said something – horrid.

– Well, what do you have to say?

The girl is totally unnerved by my one-person uprising.

– Sorry, Jenny …

– Okay, will you be friends with Princess, now?

The teacher asks it nicely. The circle of kids hold their breath. It's the tensest moment in some of their lives but it isn't the worst in mine.

– No.

– You won't be friends with her?

– No. I won't be friends with her ever again.

A girl to the right of Princess almost faints. Princess is frozen. She stares at me open-mouthed. For the first time in her life she is feeling other people's little glances at her. She looks frantic. Kind of trapped. I feel good though. Relaxed. It's the first time I've told anyone to fuck off properly in my entire life. We play music with total abandon that day. All of us kids with our sharp little teeth. Wild things! Feet that can thud, thud, thud on the floor. Hands to beat hard on the tom-tom drums.

What is better than hanging out with a puppy?

23

It is gala day today. All the kids are dressed up and on floats (which is when they decorate lorries and then drive them all through the local village), we wave at people as we drive by and there is bunting strung up from lamp posts and houses all decorated with bright paper flower garlands that spell out each kid's name above their door. I am a flower girl. My adopted mum spent ages crinkling up flowers with crêpe paper for my skirt so I could go on the lorry. She seemed to like that. It was really nice to see her happy for a whole day. The lorries come right into the caravan park to pick everyone up. The fair comes into town this week too and all the teenagers snog each other and get pished and go on rides. There are travellers, then there are tinkers, gypsies, Romanies, there are New Age travellers who make LSD for the high-school kids, and then there are static year-round caravan parks for people like us. I was playing with the traveller kids in our park last week and the man in charge of the site came over and shouted.

– You are not meant to be in here, go on, get lost.

– Why aren't they allowed to play here?

– Because they are gypsies, Jenny.

– They aren't actually, they're travellers, and what's the difference really? We're just lazy gypsies, we don't move anywhere!

He was raging.

I stole a packet of biscuits from his shop. It's cos I am hungry. All the time! I steal food and live in mortal fear of being caught. Anyway! I changed my name so it is spelled with an i now. I think about my real name sometimes but I never tell anybody that I used to be called a whole different thing and I wasn't even this person and that I've had different last names too and I don't have a birth certificate. All the kids on the floats ahead of us are waving at everyone as we go through town. Prizes are awarded for the best float. The Girl Guides have a float, the BBs, the Scouts, and the Miners' Club and all the other local clubs too. We drive slow through town and there is music and everyone is smiling and later we will all go to the old folks' home cos they like to see us dressed up and when it's over they wave at us all happy as we go away!

24

Miss Johnson in primary is waving a Bible around.

– What are you going to be when you grow up?

– I don't know, Miss!

A little boy who is smaller than everyone else is already close to tears.

She's picking us off one by one.

– Jenni?

– Miss?

– What are you going to be when you grow up?

– I'm going to be a witch.

– What?

Kids snigger. Sit up a bit straighter. I pull my elbows off the table. Miss Johnson assesses me – one hand on her Bible. The bossy Princess girl is helpless at my answer. She wants to be an Olympic gymnast and she probably will be and then we will all have to see her in the magazines constantly being an outrageous cunt about her thinness and her fitness and her money, and her fucking dumb face will follow me forever. The other kids laugh. I don't care. I don't want to be world-famous or super fit and I don't need everyone to cheer for me – I just want to spell cast and ride a broomstick; it's not even an impractical ambition.

– That doesn't sound very Christian, does it, Jenni?

– No?

– No! Pick something else!

– Fine, I'll be a coal miner then …

– You can't be a coal miner because they won't let women do that and there is no such thing as witches, so I am going to ask you one last time, what do you want to be when you grow up, Jenni?

– I want to be a writer!

There, I've said what I want to be and this clearly wasn't what she expected me to say – I look back at her slow-blinking tortoise eyes and we all just sit there awkward as fuck for a good long minute.

– I see.

When it comes to witchcraft, or words, Miss Johnson doesn't know a fucking thing.

I was born like this.

I tried for hours to move a pencil using just my eyes.

Didn't move a fucking inch.

It's so annoying.

There is a light in me that has such force, though, it is actually hard to stay still, or go to sleep. I really struggle to go to sleep every night. It's not just the horrible shrinking feeling when I close my eyes and feel like I'm back in a black box of a room. Humans don't use most of our brains so telepathy and telekinesis are just parts we need to work on and one day we will use those energies and it will just be normal. People can be more than we are. I know it. I can literally feel energy off people – like dust spiralling through light, we breathe in each other's atoms. Miss Johnson is now questioning other kids but she has steady disapproval fixed towards me. When someone is this mean I try to think about a nice thing. Like how I had a sleepover at my best friend's last weekend and it was the best time. I love staying over at her place and her mum cooks different things and we get to stay up and watch films and it is just always the happiest part of my week and I go to hers a lot now. We went to see her friend who lives in a posh house this time. People with money have carpets that smell way better. We all just chatted and hung out in her huge living room on fancy sofas and we didn't really do much but somehow it was still everything. Later, when we were going to sleep, I made up stories for my best friend until she fell asleep and it was good to know she could dream safe and happy, sometimes it is more like we are sisters than friends. I wish I could protect her from everything.

25

One of the teenagers who told me all about telekinesis last week is sitting at the swings and smoking a joint. She hands it to me. It stinks. I am hoping it won't burn me. I take a long drag and don't cough or everyone will talk about me being a fucking baby.

– Do you feel stoned, Jenni?

– Nope.

– Do you feel happier?

– Maybe.

– You're high.

– No, I'm not.

– Is this the first time you've smoked, Jenni?

– No.

– When was the first time?

– When I was six …

– That's young! How come?

– I was in a caravan around the corner and the older kids made me smoke a cigarette to see if I knew how to do it right or if I'd start coughing.

– Did you?

– No. I smoked it. Whole thing.

– Wow. You should try magic mushrooms soon too. Do you want another drag?

– Okay.

Kids often trust me a lot. They tell me stuff I don't want to know. Like some really bad things I can't ever say again.

People who are dead. Who got hurt. Then they tell me to not repeat it so I don't. Or someone's brother who has been doing it to them since they were little and their parents probably even know. I hated that so much. Or someone's mum making them touch them, or someone with a dog, or a horse, or someone who blew themselves up one day because their son touched kids. Or the mum up the back who does porn in her garden while her husband films it and the boys all hide so they can wank at the fence. The older boys here say the phrase – old enough to bleed old enough to breed.

I have actual tits now and I have to wear a bra and I fucking hate it.

Go up to my pal's caravan cos my adopted mum is working so I've to wait there and I really don't feel well.

Maybe the joint!

My stomach hurts. I feel so fucking ill. I remember this one time a social worker came to the caravan and put up a flow-chart in the living room and used a marker pen to draw a cat, then on the other side of the paper she sketched out a lion.

– Where some people might see a cat, Jenni …

She pointed with her pen.

– Uh-huh?

– Your biological mother would not see a cat, she would see a lion.

A sharp intake of breath …

– That's so cool!

All of the adults glanced at each other.

– No, it's not good because she might be frightened by the lion.

I said damn later that day by accident. I had been thinking about my real mum being able to see things that other people can't and also the books I love most and I'd said it out loud – my adopted mum dragged me into the kitchen, shoved my head in the sink and poured Fairy Liquid into my mouth until my eyes were watering and it tasted so disgusting I wanted to cry all night. She didn't seem to care in the slightest. Then yesterday I got caught taking a spoonful of icing sugar from the cabinet in the living room. I must have left a dust trail and she saw it. When I got home from school I asked what was for tea.

– Icing sugar.

– I don't want it.

– Well, you wanted it before, Jenni, didn't you? When you were stealing it, didn't you want it then? Go on, look in the living room.

There was a bowl of icing sugar and a spoon on the table.

It's the level of hatred that gets you.

I hurt constantly. I am hurt. I feel weak. Faint. I want to go to sleep and just not wake up. Nothing feels good about me. I hate myself. I try to starve myself as much as I can. A feeling in the back of my mind tells me I should not be made to feel like this. That I don't deserve it. That I could change my story altogether. That I could be free. I drop loo roll into the pan and it has bright red blood all over it. I can't believe I'm only nine years old and I've just got my period.

26

When someone asks what I do at the weekend, I don't say
chores then my adopted mum scours out the inside of my mind
with a Brillo pad to dull the bits that dare to shine. Sometimes
we go to my adopted mother's parents at the weekend and they
have a piano room, and I sit and play it for hours and her mum
makes home-made scones and salads with stuff picked out the
garden and fresh strawberries and they are always nice to me,
really they are, but I don't ever feel like I know them. I'm going
over to the dump this weekend and I won't be saying that at
school on Monday. Go by a caravan that stinks so bad; some
kids are out on the porch eating sugar sandwiches, I just say
hi and keep going. Then I see the older girl who stuck her fat
tongue down my neck when I was about six and was always
trying to force us to do things and I wondered one day how
she knew about all that stuff or what was being done to her
but I still hated her and she knew it. Then one time she told
me about that really short dwarf guy who moved in and was
caught buzzing from a Calor Gas canister outside his caravan
with another guy and she said when the police went in they
had enough explosives and weapons to blow up the city. That
was just a few caravans away. I run out onto the farmland and
down the edge of the fields so the farmer won't see me and
then across the road and stealth-creep into the dump so the
diggers won't see me. It's so vast in here. So stark! Things flap
in the wind and it stinks. I crunch over broken glass and step
on a load of old tyres to see what is new today. It smells of

spilled petrol and rotten eggs. Seagulls caw and swoop across half-open suitcases. The ground is strewn with torn letters and wet clothes and old medicine bottles. Bend down to read one. Shake the bottle. No pills in it. Head for the cliffs. Huge vast things made entirely of mulched paper. They are as high as two houses. That leap! I want that moment where I am suspended in the air like a photograph caught in full colour! All of the kids that play in the dump probably have a million diseases going through us. Our eyes glow yellow in the dark. I find a little fridge and tip it up. Stand in front of a mannequin who only has one arm and a line of blue drawn above her eyes and blonde plastic hair.

The mannequin looks blankly at me.

I don't try to do a dance routine today. I used to do them with my ghetto blaster over at the waste ground and I'd dream of running away to live in New York and never coming back here ever again. Imagine getting to go to New York one day! That would be so amazing. I am going to do it no matter what I have to survive just to get there. I slide down a pile of rubble. Find a jar of buttons. Open it and throw them at the sky. Stalk my way across the dump like I am on the catwalk in Milan wearing haute couture!

I slide down the hill right at the top of the tallest paper cliffs feeling a buzz already.

No digger trucks nearby!

Run as fast as I can and then just … leap!

I hated the mullet, tried to grow it out.

27

The word they use on the news is recession. It's said all the time. What it means is people in poverty are dying while rich people think they are vermin. The effect is tangible in a lot of the caravans around here, and up in the village too. We don't have much money and she always goes on about being poor but we do have food, and electricity, just nothing extra. Most of my clothes are from the jumble sale, or the cheap shop in town, and we don't have a car or take holidays, and my adopted mother says that she wishes she could afford to buy fruit, but they are both working and they smoke and she has a massive wardrobe with all her fake-fur coats that she likes to stride out in when visiting her parents on a Sunday (it embarrasses me so much to be next to someone wearing any kind of fur), so we aren't quite as skint as lots of people who literally can't buy anything at all. I go into some caravans and they are so cold, they smell of damp, cheap tinned food, dirty microwaves, worn carpets and generational despair. I keep going until I get to my best friend's caravan. Go up three creaky wooden steps and knock on the metal door. There is a light on inside. Her dad opens the door and he is wearing overalls with oil on them – always. I go in and he moves a stack of car manuals and makes a cup of tea and I sit on the sofa. Their dog Tramp comes to sit by our feet. Tramp is the best dog, he is so smart and friendly. My best pal has on a Mickey Mouse jumper. It is reversible. I have one too. They sell them at Bonnyrigg market. We sit and watch telly and chat and I am happy – in that caravan – just us three – I'm allowed to stay for tea and he doesn't know what to cook cos he's not always so good at things like that. He has a big nose and fuzzy hair that could be white or grey and he never talks to us like we are kids – he talks to us like we are equals in some way. I go into the fridge and find honey and a can of spray cream and there are bananas, and some chocolate so I grate that and do a made-up pudding for us. I make meals just out of this or that and it's always an adventure and usually tastes good and we laugh, we really, really laugh, and when I go back later that night the bit of me that shines – that has always done so – is a tiny bit stronger again.

Later that will go.

I know to make sure it isn't seen.

I was allowed to go to the school disco. Very unusual! When I get home they are sat in the living room with a suitcase between them.

– Is everything okay?

– We are having a family meeting, go to your room.

I go through to my room and wonder why I am not part of a family meeting. It's cos the family is them. It always was. Then there is me. I write poetry in my diary. He is going to leave. It will just be me and her then. It's cold in my room. Flick through my diary and old poems and then, also, little stories. Imagine if one day I wrote books. Alice in Wonderland believes six impossible things before breakfast so I can believe one. I write poems about everything. Nobody will ever read them. I don't tell anyone really. Mrs Kite in school got me to read out one of my stories to the class though – she says I am the best reader because I go slowly so each character comes alive and at the end she stood in front of everyone and said she was totally certain that one day she was going to walk into a bookshop and find a novel with my name on the spine.

It is the nicest, kindest thing anyone ever said to me.

I get into bed. I reach for my glow-worm. If you squeeze his stomach then he lights up from his head down into his body. He has a green soft set of worm rings and his head glows yellow. I go all the way under the covers and open my old favourite. The Dark Riders are coming. The Hobbits must get away from them. Nostrils flare and horse hooves pound the ground. The Hobbits get so many different things to eat even on the road – they find a tavern and order a pint and smoke pipe weed and then much, much later, they are guided to Elvish town, one of the Elvish queen's daughters turns up to guide them and she has pointy ears and straight hair and she can turn the entire river into water horses so the Dark Riders can't follow. I put the book down when my hand gets numb from clutching the glow-worm. When she grounded me all the time I'd read two or three books a day. Do chores then just sit in this room reading book after book. I want to be Elvish. Chatter in tongues and write in their language. When I go into a book the unbearable hideousness of life is left outside. Traces of it can't be shaken off though. My fingers get cold. So does my nose. Hunger still bites. A residue of anger from being shouted at too long. To counter all of it, I go further into the world of a book. I get so far into the story that when I look over my shoulder there are miles and miles of the Shire between me and the caravan and I can smell pipe weed and a smoke ring in the shape of a ship drifts right across my room. Nobody shouts at me in this world for shining, because in here – light is sacred.

At my friend's birthday.

28

She makes me pull my play trousers down. Smacks my bare arse hard. It has happened quite a lot lately. I am so big now that this is ridiculous. Designed only to shame me. She seems to look for new ways to do that. I begin to think she gets some kind of a buzz from it. The humiliations, the constant dressing-downs, the little wounds nobody else can see. She said I had to take my pants down because a bare arse feels more pain. A slap sounds louder that way. It makes my skin crawl. Little goosebumps go up all over my arms. I hide everything. Bad things. Anger. Sadness. My emotions seem to repel her. She does not feel empathy for me. She is the victim of the bad child! Such an ungrateful child! I learned the word empathy when I was seven. I rolled it around in my mouth. I have it. It's in me. I hurt when other people do. Pain and distress really gets to me even if it isn't me that's feeling it. I still don't tell anyone I read the dictionary, it's bad enough being a scaff living in a caravan with a mother that makes me look as ugly as she can nearly all the time. She wants to take me down all the pegs, she uses her words to hang me up by the skin. She sees a soft spot and she is in there and then tells me it's my fault she had to do it. I'm lucky my friends at school like me because she makes me wear only two possible looks – antique doll, or a total fucking tregg, as shan as anyone could be. I go past her bedroom – there is a frilly bedspread and so many teddy bears and dolls. I catch sight of myself in the mirror. Shiny hair; my skin is bare as a doll. Step into her room quiet. There is a wall of wardrobes stuffed with her clothes. She has so many. Hundreds, way, way more than he has, or I ever will. It's like she is playing at dressing-up, but she wants me to be as dowdy as she can make me. It's like she's pretending to be a grown-up but she is just an angry, jealous, bitter, cruel child. Open a wardrobe door. Her clothes are bright colours. Vivid cerise-pink long skirt with a diagonal cut. Bright belts. Fake-fur coats, or maybe some are real. High heels. She wears bright blue eyeshadow. It is like we must all look at her all the time or what? What will happen if we don't? The dolls will set us on fire. I go around to the other side of the bed where his things are. There is a massive stack of porn magazines. I take the top one off. He must buy them from the site shop. The women have things in their mouths. Gags. Leather or things like that. It is nearly all small pictures. All her teddies look straight ahead. The dolls keep their prim little hands by their sides. Their neat petticoats are white, or their velvet coats, or dresses, cared for so precisely and diligently … yet I have to go out to play in cut-off jumble-sale trousers with rags hanging at the bottom that don't even fit me. I put the porn magazines back carefully. I suppose they're there because she doesn't sleep with him. Yet, she still sits around the house naked watching telly at night sometimes. It is so fucking bizarre! She says she likes air to get into her skin. When she does that, he looks straight ahead at the telly and I just want to be sick. I tiptoe back out of their room. My hair smells of Vosene shampoo. She is always saying how we are so poor and she is so hard done to in every way but she won't stop smoking even although it stinks and it is expensive. She says it's her only vice and treat and pleasure. Her dolls, and teddies, and wardrobe, and box of sugared almonds, they all say something different. They are not the same kind of poor that lots of the other kids' families in this caravan park are, even although they do struggle a lot, still, they do also have some things other people don't. I am to cost as little as possible though. If she puts diluting juice in my water, though it is just a tiny drop, it barely flavours it. She didn't grow up like this. Her parents have a nice house with a garden where they grow strawberries and fresh vegetables and a big bathroom and upstairs bedrooms and a cool old attic off the stairs that I climb into and go and look for treasure. They have a grandfather clock that ticks in the hallway. A really nice living room and another front room where the piano is too. Her dad was in the army. Her mum has the neatest figure and she always wears a twin set and pearls. Her mum makes fresh pancakes when we visit or brings out a three-tier plate with French fancies on it. I used to like to sit with her parents and play *Countdown* off the telly. I don't often get maths right but I do well in word games. I love those. They let me stay there when I was wee one night and I said I wanted to pray because I don't know where I come from and they let me and they understood why I wanted to and I slept in a bed that was so clean with all the different sheets and heavy blankets. I got to sit in the garden for a while. They would make dinner with bread sauce and roast potatoes but soup first when it was cold outside. I remember her mum saying to her she had to stop being so constantly harsh with me. Nobody knows most of it! Only what they see when she snaps at me in front of them. She doesn't care what anyone thinks about her. God himself could come down right now and tell her the way she talks to me is worse than cruel and she'd just tear a strip off him and go after me ten times harder when he left. She is completely convinced of her own rightness, above all people, at every single second.

It's not even night-time but I am so cold I am going to bed. Don't feel like I can even pretend to be okay any more today. I'll jump out if I hear her coming.

Get under my covers.

Read and read and read.

Life feels like being eaten alive whole by a fucking snake lately. I still don't sleep. I always check under the bed before I close my eyes. Sometimes I do it twice, or three times. It's only a matter of time. I shrink when I'm falling asleep. My tongue expands in my mouth and it is the most horrible feeling. And this person from my earliest past who I've been afraid of my whole life is still out there – going through all the front doors – looking for me.

29

She said she was going to commit suicide at Hogmanay. When I got back from a holiday in the Highlands with my best friend's family after that, I found my adopted dad had come back like he hadn't gone away at all. Like I hadn't been made to take her wedding rings back to him in an envelope and hand them over in a greasy spoon at the bus station one Saturday. Like I didn't do all the food shopping and everything else cos she'd broke her ankle or turned her leg or whatever it was that meant she couldn't walk right for months. Now my adopted mum talks to me coldly and politely like I'm a lodger. I trudge out in the snow. Go around to the park next door. I'm going to make a huge snowman in the dark. I start by patting a single snowball until it is totally solid. Then roll it lightly in huge lines up and down the park in fresh snow. It ends up so big I have to use my whole body to push it along. I leave a furrow of bare snow with scraps of grass poking through behind me. Then I do the head. Settle it super carefully so it doesn't fall off. If it stays cold enough my snowman could be here for a week. Stones for eyes and a carrot for his nose. There are dark hills behind his twig arms. I look at all the lights going on in the caravans and smells of cooking waft down and different television shows crackle in the night air. My snowman is pretty brilliant. Chuffed with him. Snowflakes begin to fall gently.

Tip my head back and open my mouth and let them land on my tongue.

Open my arms out.

Spin myself around faster and faster and faster until I fall down.

The trees all bare and twiggy.

Witch-like!

Jagged.

I'm scared of her, that is true. I've wondered what is wrong with her so many times to make her so angry or just to feel no empathy, not for me anyway. There isn't anything though. That's what she says, she is just how she is, and the person who gets the worst of it is me. Some people are one person to you then different to nearly everyone else. I try to think of ways that she is good. Like how she says nobody should discriminate against people for being gay, or black, or brown. I can like that about her. It is so racist in some places here. A local Asian family working in the village had a shit posted through their door and it made me feel so sick that anyone can act like that and I wanted to scream. It is literally disgusting. People can be so utterly fucking horrid! You go to a friend's parents' house sometimes and they say racist stuff just to see if you will react because they instinctively know you think they are fucking idiots for being racists and they don't like it at all. They think you are dumb, or up yourself, for not thinking like them. They dislike you for it. The older boys are always looking to see which girls have big tits. They want a diddy ride. They want a slag. They say this girl is a bike and that one is frigid. They say some girls are colder than a witch's tit, or they say she is asking for it. You hear that a lot. She's asking fir it! I don't want a woman's body. I didn't ask for it. I want to be straight up and down with no curves. I made my snowman fat and round though. I'm still hungry all the time. I try to find things to eat that she won't notice but there isn't really anything. Maybe an old tin of Spam or something. It's rank. Or hundreds and thousands tipped straight onto the tongue. Sometimes I have a piece of bread with tomato ketchup on it. I panic then that she will notice. I've never felt good about eating one thing in my entire life. I think about when she'd make me put my hands out waiting to get smacked, or that I had to bend over, she'd tell me she was going to do it and I had to go through that horrible moment where time elongated and she knew that waiting was the worst bit. The world spinning a little faster than it had done a minute before. The glass doors through to the kitchen, the glass dining table with metal tubes holding it up and me every day cleaning, or sorting the kitchen out, hoovering and ironing and walking the dog and cutting wood sometimes, or going to the shops, putting away the dishes, scrubbing food off the cooker and making my bed, hanging up the washing, walking the dog again and going to get bread and pulling weeds out the path and peeling vegetables and folding clothes away and years ago helping when she fostered disabled kids and she liked them a lot more than she did me, they didn't get any of this, to be fair I think she likes everyone more than she likes me, and so I just keep taking the anger which lashes off her every fucking day.

I wish one day she'd see I'm really not that bad.

I get all good results at school, I work as hard as I can, my friends think I'm funny, I am decent, so what is this awful thing that makes her just fucking hate me? It's never going to change. I lie down on the snow next to my snowman. Scissor my legs and arms to make an angel. I get up and make another one, leave angels all over the park, and in the last one I just lie there and stare up at the stars coming out in the sky – snow swirls down and I feel clean and happy for a minute because this world is really so, so beautiful.

30

The stars are old and dead. The light we see comes to us from a long time ago. Still, how they shine! We walk by two little cottages with a warm yellow glow in their windows, then past the farm road, then fields and a hulk of hills in the distance. I wonder if the wild cat still roams those hills. Or maybe a wolf. That's not likely but I love to think of them out in the wild somewhere in the world – one day I want to hear them howling at the moon. Every year we do this same midnight walk. It is the only time I feel we are at peace. We make it up to the miners' hall with its brightness and hot breath and steam and damp clothes and file our way through in time for the little kids' choir to start singing. Sit at the back. The two villages around us are both mining areas. There is still plenty of community here even if the pits are closed now. A lot of people here look out for each other too, especially since the poverty got so much worse for nearly everyone. We all turned out to watch the big wheels stop turning on the coal mines. I will never forget how silent everyone was that day. While we all sing carols the old floor stains wet from snow melting on welly boots. Outside it grows even crisper and clearer. It is a nice few hours in our life together. I wish it could be like this even just a little bit more. It is a different world when she is calm and happy and not mad at me. It's best to just hold on to a good moment while it's here. I am so tired though. I sing the songs just like I always have but I don't smile any more.

Something has gone from me.

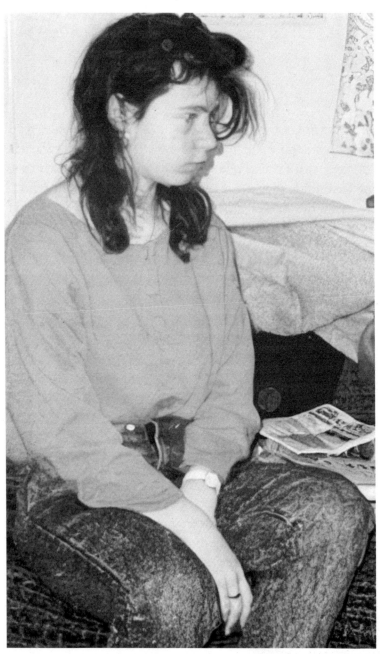

Just don't even know how to act okay any more.

31

I don't know exactly when I decided to do it. A long time ago. Maybe when I was born. Someone once told me about an African fable that says when a child is treated too harshly their soul retreats from their body and does not come back until it is safe to do so and if there is no break then I guess the soul just doesn't come back at all.

My soul lives in the other world.

It leaves my body here.

I am so homesick for a place I don't know.

People I've never seen.

Arms that won't hold me even once in my life.

Words that will not be said at any point and rescuers who are not coming for me.

I can't take any more.

The older kids in the caravan park want me to give someone a blow job. It's so gross. I don't want to even kiss anyone. They stink and they say I'll need to do it soon. I am not into it. I remember when I was little and some older boys at school kept pulling up the girls' skirts to see their pants. I told on them and they said I was a prude. I didn't give a shit. My pants were none of their fucking business. I don't want to be here any more with people thinking cos I look like a woman I should be doing that pish. They got me to sit on someone's knee the other night and I hated every second of it. They thought it was funny. The smell of sex everywhere – like a burnt match – I didn't like it. I've looked like this since I was nine and now I'm twelve it's harder to keep them away. Some girls in high school don't like me cos of the attention maybe. I hate it. Cos I'm a grade-A student in nearly everything too. Or maybe they just hate me and there is no other reason. They have begun to lay into me with their cut and jibe every day lately. Looks in the corridor become insults in the classroom. Veiled threats. I exude something they don't like. Not all of them! I have friends and a boy I hung out with for a while but I didn't want to be his girlfriend. I just want to smoke cigarettes and swear and maybe let a boy kiss me just so I can work out if I am a true lesbian or not. I don't think I can go through being bullied in high school. It feels like I've been bullied or worse in so many placements and at primary and at home and I just can't take it happening again. I still write poetry in secret. I won third prize in a writing competition in a library on a council estate. That was pretty amazing. Picked up my award (book tokens for James Thin's) wearing a purple knitted skirt and polo neck that for once I actually loved. My adopted parents were proud of me that day. I do my school projects at a cold table and make them look pretty and a little hole appears in the corner of my bedroom floor one time and it has to be filled with something so field mice don't get in when winter comes, not that the cats wouldn't kill them anyway. I learned sign language really well from my babysitter. I practise the alphabet on my fingers often. I still go to the disabled kids' support groups, who my adopted mum volunteers with – their discos and clubs are on every year – so I know how great those kids are and also how lucky I am to be able to move my body around easily and why I shouldn't take it for granted. She is good with all those kids, it is just something that she hates about me.

I am going to go crazy one day just like my real mother.

We all know it.

I have bad thoughts all the time now.

There is a bully in my brain that won't be happy until it kills me.

Every direction is bad right now and even things I used to like do not feel safe any more.

I slowly close the orange curtains in my bedroom.

Step back and just stand in that room totally still for a minute making sure. Get my record player ready. It has four different coloured lights that flash to the beat. I've danced to so many records on my own in here. To old fifties songs about T-birds and libraries and a boyfriend coming back and death metal records on clear floppy vinyl cut out in squares from magazines by friends' older brothers, and then cut into circles and given to me on loan and I'd mosh my head to those and I heard a preview snippet of a soundbite from 'Little Fluffy Clouds' on the radio in here and was fucking transported! I carefully place a record on my turntable, needle poised ...

They are both out tonight.

Since he came home she acts like a polite stranger. A new tactic! It is what it is. I've not allowed thoughts of anyone I love into my mind for a long time. They will be okay. I'm totally sure of it. Through to the living room. Into the drinks cabinet, heartbeat picks up. I have to move fast. Before they are back. I am terrified in case she finds me doing this. I'd be so fucking dead. Find a bottle of Malibu. It's still sticky around the base from a New Year party. Take a long sweet sickly swig. Straight into her medicine box. This has to be done properly. I am far more afraid of what will happen if I survive after she finds out what I've done than I am of dying. This is not a call for help. Nobody can help me. That is already very clear in my life. I am not looking for attention. This has to work. I count out tablets.

Ten for pain. No, fifteen at least, then six for angina, possibly eight, okay, four more of those makes twelve on top of fifteen, is that maths right? Strips of paracetamol crackle as I pop out all the tablets. Force them down! It is hard to swallow so many tablets! My eyes water. Throat burns! I work methodically, quickly and precisely – as I have learned to do with everything. My mouth tastes of chemicals. The whole world tilts to the left. Slug down more Malibu. Descend to a place three levels lower than my usual world. I take the last tablet. Have to force myself to swallow repeatedly to get it down. My throat is closing up. I put the Malibu back, carefully. Tidy so they won't see anything when they come in. Begin to panic! What have I done? What if I don't really want to die? It's too late now. I don't even know if dying this way will be painful. Float through to my room. Drop the needle on the record. Lie down. A big gospel choir sings to me. Everything spins! I am never even going to be a teenager. I'm always going to be a virgin. Thoughts lace together like paper chains across the classroom when I was a little kid and there are memories on each of them. Look at my bedroom wall where I had a nightmare about a giant shark coming to eat me when I first moved here – its jaws open so wide they swallowed my entire room!

It won't be long now.

I can feel it, high and woozy, lying in the dark knowing I am going to die – no point to struggling, I just have to go with it and sink down into this feeling, and I can't actually move any more and the record ends and makes a pffffft, pfffffft, pffffffft sound as the lights on my speakers flash red and then yellow, green and … blue.

32

Lurch upwards. Soaked in sweat. Levitate. A plague of rats gnaw through raw flesh, this is more pain than is even possible for a human to bear. My guts! Pass out. Light drags me back up. It must be morning. The room is an orange glow. Crawl to the bathroom. Kneel on a towelled loo mat. Project burning hot acidic chemical vomit over and over, flush. My whole body convulses. Retch over and over – until there is red flesh spattered across the white bowl. That must be my stomach. Cold sweats! Dark comes. Pass out! Wake in a haze of pain. Throw up my stomach lining! It is excruciating. It won't be much longer now. Nobody can survive this. It's inhuman. I can feel my organs closing down. I hear her lighter spark as she wakes next door.

A hit of smoke.

Snarling through the wall …

– That's what you get for eating too many sweeties.

Inspect the pink-red lumps of flesh in the toilet.

Vomit again, tears, heat, fading, sick, so weak, and she is at the door then – her face pales when she sees me. She gets me up off the floor. I'm almost dead now, it can't be long, I am desperate to go – this pain is too much to bear. She is asking things and I tell her I had a headache maybe, I took a painkiller, there is a phone call and her smoking in her dressing gown with the frilly high neck and all of her dolls have marched through the wall to screech at me as high and loud as they can and they point with glittering angry stares and it is dark then.

A light shone in my eyes as they are prised open.

There is a person in green, and another, and a stretcher.

I am wheeled out from the caravan strapped down flat on my back and I can hear the wheels rattle and the engine running – looking up at the bluest sky.

33

The ambulance closes its doors. Everything is metal. Metal wheels. Metal sun, metal instruments, metal heart clunk-clink. So freezing! There are steel instruments and tubes and needles. Clink. Clink. Clink. The sound of wheels is a burrrrrrr. A rubber mask is placed over my face. Someone shouts. I am going! There is motion around me. The ambulance drives out the caravan park. A loud siren blares. The pain is so agonising no human can bear it much longer than this. It will be soon. I separate from my body, rise up, the motion of the vehicle is so loud and the blue light flashes round and round and round and the siren wails. It wails and wails. Blackness finally rushes in.

I'm gone.

34

I am in a room. It is bright. I am on an operating bed with no sheets on it. There are people. They are dressed in white. They rush around. There is a machine. It beeps. I am in so much pain it is impossible to understand how a human heart stays beating through this. I keep blacking out. I disappear to a tiny dot. In the corner of my eye I see my adopted dad. He is gripping my thumb. He is pressing it as hard as he can to make sure I hear him when he says – hold on. Next to him … through a smaller circle of vision her face is so, so angry! I better die soon. Because if I don't – she is definitely going to kill me.

The lights go …

35

First there is a feeling. It is far away for a long time. I try to work out what it is. After so many days and hours in the darkness I realise it is pain. It's at the top of each of my hands. Just above my knuckles. Opening my eyes is not easy. It hurts. It takes a lot of effort. This is such a bright place. I wince. Light dazzles with trails of colour. Look down to see where the pain is other than my stomach. There is a long needle right up into my veins in both hands, which are bandaged to two long pieces of wooden board. Clear tubes snake into the needles. Two bags of fluid sit on machines either side of my body. It drips into my body. A machine beeps next to me. I have been a long way from here. There was a choice given to me in the other world. Can still feel the imprint of that place on me. It's a warmth. I got to make a decision whether to come back, or not. What I have chosen is to come back and live through things even worse than what I already chose to leave behind. I know that. I also know I made this entire choice long before I was born. It is a soul contract. If I don't see it through I will be sent here again. I was somewhere else for a while and it was so beautiful! I do know now with utter certainty that suicide isn't how any of us are meant to die though; if we can manage to not do it, what we are meant to do is follow the yellow brick road until someone else ticks that it's our time to get off.

I am not the person I was before my long sleep.

Don't know how many days have passed.

Time is different in the other place.

Can't see anything other than big white curtains closing off my bed.

Noises fade in.

Light and shapes, footsteps, a child talks to someone, a trolley rattles. As everything gets louder the other place I've been in all this time recedes. I am scared without it near me. It's where I come from. Not here! Somebody is standing as a silhouette on the other side of the curtain. My mouth tastes so strongly of chemical tablets. I want to be sick but my stomach will rarely let me do that – again for the rest of my life. I know that with certainty. I have barely been able to be sick my entire childhood. That switch got broke in me a long time ago. The overdose is the first time I can actually remember vomiting since I was very little. I want to check under my bed. Count the curtain rings. My feet are still down there at the end of my legs. Aren't they? At the bottom of the bed! Further up there are lumps where my knees are and a dip where my stomach is and a woman walks through the curtains and jumps. Then a huge warm smile. Pure! Like sunshine. She is happy to see me. I am so relieved – I cannot speak.

– We didn't know when you'd join us again!

The nurse tucks my bedsheet in and then adjusts one of the fluid bags and my blood runs up the clear tube and unfurls in the clear bag – slow and bright and red.

– Oops, don't you worry about that, it happens, don't you worry about anything. Can you speak yet?

I am too tired to even shake my head.

– You just sleep.

Wake at teatime. Someone has pulled the curtains halfway open. I am on a children's ward. Lots of little kids (and their parents) inspect me suspiciously. I am a lot bigger than every other child in here. A nurse appears. She is so warm and kind.

There is a trolley, my temperature gets taken, the nurse checks fluids in each of the bags.

– How long was I …?

– Too long. You're back now though.

I am.

Eye the ward.

There are cards and families and motion around every bed but mine, which is awkward because the other kids' parents are noticing that as well.

– They are not going to visit you, they don't want to – she said to say that they didn't want to encourage your behaviour so they won't come in to see you while you're in here.

I can tell the nurse is not happy to be passing this on.

– Okay.

– Will we try and sit you up then?

I am held under my arms as two of them lift me easily so my legs slide up the bed. I can see things better. It's good that my adopted mother isn't coming in here to kill me in front of everybody, it would be traumatising for the children. I do not doubt the anger on her face, the last thing I saw before I blacked out … will only get worse. I make a decision before they even refill the clear bags.

– I can't go back.

– What?

– They need to send me somewhere else to live.

She nods.

All the nurses seem to know without me telling them a thing.

They are so bloody nice to me!

I couldn't be more grateful.

The next morning they help me to stand up after breakfast and it feels so strange. I have to walk slowly and wobbly, with one holding my arm in my paper gown. In the other hand I pull along my machine, it comes with me on rollers and it goes bleep, bleep, bleep. I want to try and go to a toilet on my own. Not the little paper box they put under me. I don't know how long it has been since I've eaten. I am embarrassed to be seen in front of these kids with families. They get me to sit in the kids' area for a few minutes to see how I go. My legs are big long things on the tiny kid chair. I am Alice after the blue tablet, and all the other tablets, and there is no Cheshire Cat and nor is there any place like home and the yellow brick road has no red sparkling shoes on it clicking those heels and I am in a paper gown about to faint. They help me back up the ward. I am tucked into bed clean and neat. I comb my hair and sit and try to look like I am not a freak. I listen to hospital radio and try to bring my mood up and act brave and I feel very, very lonely and stupid and weak. I am also certain I could not have taken any more of what had been building in me probably since before I was even born. A psychiatrist ambles down the ward. He is old and weird and stinks of chocolate and even more vaguely of shit. I wonder if he is the kind of person who would molest me. He definitely looks like he would. I don't want to be on my own with him.

– How are you this morning then, Jenni?

– I can't go back.

– I know, and your adopted family said that they don't want you back. You will have to go back to the caravan park of course, just for one or two days to pack your things, and then you are to go into a placement, we have found a foster family who will take you, they have two daughters of their own and one other foster child.

Nod.

– Have you eaten yet?

– No.

He marks things on the pad at the end of my bed and says things but all I hear is that I can go somewhere else. I am on my own in the world again. Soon, I am strong enough to try walking outside. I go to wait for the nurse at the front door because she is walking me up and down the Meadows each afternoon to try and get me used to being on my feet again. I feel shaky. Guys in blue scrubs smoke in the doorway.

– Could I please, please have one of those?

– Aye, go on then, here.

I am blessed with one Regal King Size and two matches to hide. Who says there are no such things as angels?!

36

The nurse helps me in the outside world. Her hand is kindly steadying me by holding my arm. Some people are so good it makes you feel stronger just to be near them. There are trees in the park. People sit having picnics or drinking beer, chatting, kicking a ball around. There is a whale bone at the end of Middle Meadow Walk. I look up at birds, watch children laughing, dogs pounding around just ecstatic to be in a park, and the grass is bright green in the sunlight. It's like I have just arrived back on earth. It is as strange and beautiful as any place could be. We go into the shady bit between the trees. She lets me stop for a little while. Students sit around chatting. Someone drums somewhere. There are people on bicycles and I am here, I am here! I am still alive. I am me! I am free! I will be going somewhere new and I won't have to go back to how my life was before. I am not going to do this to myself ever again, I know that as well, even if I really want to. My suicide attempt was a one-shot-only thing. It was a good effort, the best, and despite all things my body has kept going. I place one skinny foot in front of the other. I have dark bruises on my hands and red scars where the big long needles were kept in for ages. I am still not hungry for food yet. I just want this taste gone. It is so chemical and vile it seeps out of my pores. Back on the ward it is time for the doctor's visit.

– Can you see how pale she is, and she's very unresponsive still.

He hits my knee with a hammer.

Barely a flutter!

– The patient was solely on IV fluids until only two days ago …

The training medics all stare. I sit like a bag of meat in a paper dress. Wonder how long it is before I can get to a bathroom to smoke the cigarette I've hidden under my pillow.

– Jenni, they have cleaned as much from your system as possible but you will not be able to take painkillers again for a very, very long time, young lady, your stomach is severely damaged from this. Do you understand?

Nod.

Eventually they go.

It is visiting hour again.

Awkward.

I don't get visits.

I listen to hospital radio because it is embarrassing to be a suicide survivor giant child among a ward of wee kids getting their tonsils out or crayons pulled from their nose or whatever else it is most of them are in here for. I keep my eyes down but glance up for just a second to see my best friend walking down the ward towards me. Her dad is behind her. I want to cry. I am so mortified to have done this. They are looking for me and there is worry on their faces. I can't remember what they say but he can see I've not been eating.

– Can I bring you any food in?

– Pickles, just a whole jar of pickles, please!

He goes to the chippy and comes back with a white-pudding supper and chips and I can't face that yet, but I eat pickle after pickle out a jar and it is not totally enough because all I can still taste is paracetamol and angina tablets and chemicals – so, I drink the entire jar of vinegar and I am finally able to feel the taste in my mouth go away for a minute. I try not to look at my best friend too much because I've hurt her really badly.

– I'm so, so, so sorry!

I am.

I am.

I am.

I am.

I am.

I am.

I am.

I am.

I am an awful person.

I don't know why anybody wants anything to do with me.

37

Spark the match and strike it again. I have to do it twice. Sulphur flares. A tiny warm glow in the cold women's bathroom cubicle. Inhale deeply. Dizzy. Might fall over. Still unsteady on my feet at times. The nurses in here have been so nice to me. They are so kind that a part of me just wants to live here now. I feel – liked. I feel – cared for. I feel – safe.

Today I have to leave.

38

I walk back into the caravan. She wears a neutral face. I am told how it will go. Firstly – I will pack my things. Over the next two days they will be polite, as will I. A social worker will come and get me after that. I will go to live in a foster placement. I will have tea and breakfast as usual.

– Can I go and see my best friend to say goodbye?

– Yes.

Walk up the hill for the last time. Look at every stone. Paths I've walked countless times. This was my childhood home. It's not any more. Go by a garage wall. I hit a tennis ball there for hours in summer. Places I skinned my knees. Past strange or crooked caravans, or neat ones, or the one where I would run naked in a friend's garden with her when we were tiny kids in the summer. Or, the woodsmoke scent of autumn and the hills turning starker, barer, at the first frost and me always waiting on snow, for icicles to hang from the caravan window so I could snap them off and eat them. I've walked this way towards my best friend's dad's caravan thousands of times. Press down quietly on the lumps on my hands where long needles kept me alive with fluids. On the path there are other smells to catch in the cold downwind. Scrap metal. Melting tarmac to mend never-ending potholes on the roads, or to be rolled along some caravan roof to keep the rain out. Grass that has grown too long or yellowed, rain soaked that earthen way, and a rich tang of dog shit, and cooking smells, real chips frying, a Fray Bentos pie. I smell everything like I've just been given it as a gift. Things change when you come back from the other side. I am not the same. Still guilty that I hurt my friend though. It is hard to show my face. Knock on her door. Stand at the top of the three steps to her caravan. I will though. I'll say sorry. I'll keep saying it because I am. I didn't do this to hurt anybody. Walking in to see people you have hurt is the hardest thing. We sit on the sofa. Chat. It is okay, they try hard to make it be okay, but we all know it's not really. I can't take back what I did. My best friend is just a kid who doesn't understand why someone she cares so much about would leave her. I don't blame her for feeling like that. I can't explain my past, or everything else, but I can make her laugh, and we can be glad of this space and moment together because it is so precious not just to them – their care and love over all the years has meant the whole world and more to me and I will always be grateful for it.

Used to do my hair in a French plait, trying to care for me.

PART THREE

Age 12–16

39

I packed my copy of *The Hobbit*. It's in the bottom of my bag. I have my fairy-tale books. They are hidden too. We are sitting outside a semi-detached council house with a driveway and a very neat garden. This estate is nice. Everything is well kept. I bet a lot of people here have even bought their houses. My adopted mum gets out first because she wants to see where I am going and the social worker follows. The foster mother opens the door and they say hello to each other. We all go in. The adults want to talk about something in the living room so I stand in a stranger's kitchen. It feels like so much fuss! Just for me to live somewhere. I could have just slipped away. I've inconvenienced everybody. I am going to miss my granny and my adopted dad's sister always made me mixtapes and I liked her loads too and not everything was bad all the time even with my adopted folks – we laughed too – but now it's all gone. I only got those people as my family and friends when I could take what she was dealing out to me.

That was the arrangement and we all know it.

I go and they all stay silent.

Nobody ever wants to say a thing, it makes everyone feel – uncomfortable.

Best just to forget me.

Or ignore it.

Then blame me when I do say something and that overdose was the first time in my life I had ever said fuck off quite so clearly. I am grateful though, for things I did have, for all those times watching *Columbo* with my granny and baking a cake for Christmas with her or running up to my best pal's and just getting to be young, but even aside from all that I can't take away the absolute truth in me of all that pain, all those years biting my thumb, or hurting myself, or hiding every negative emotion, or taking the tongue lashing or all the rest of it, and even more than that there was something in me that she pushed and pushed and pushed and pushed and pushed and pushed and pushed – until it broke.

Childhood is over.

I'm twelve years old and it will be just me from now on.

This has all gone too far!

I begin to cry.

– Are you okay?

– I'm fine.

– Come on, sort yourself out, don't you give her the satisfaction of letting her see that she is making you upset, go on, dry your eyes.

The new foster mother disappears next door. I sort myself the fuck out. It's hard to act normal when you feel so fucking weird. I shrink then I grow big. I must try to act sane. If I act it maybe nobody will notice that I'm probably already half mental. The foster mother comes through. She has curly hair and is youngish and smiles a lot and is pretty nice really. It's such a relief when the social worker and adopted mum close the front door behind them but I also feel so awkward because this family are now stuck with me.

Go into the hall and look at the rooms from there to work out the lay of the land.

Just like I used to do … exactly, this.

– Our other foster child will be back soon – you'll be sharing a room upstairs with Minnie.

Nod and get shown around. If the new foster sister wants to fight me what do I do? I could read her a poem. One about why fighting is futile. Under my fear of violence, the real one is that in me there is a temper so bad that I better never let it out. My adopted mum thought I might grow up to be a murderer when I was only little. Imagine the other mums saying – oh what do you think they will be when they're older? Her saying – life, she'll be doing life most likely. I am scared of my shadow. I won't write a poem about that.

– Our two daughters are out just now, one is working and one is at the high school. You don't know where anything is around here, so you better not go out or you'll get lost, wait until one of our girls can show you around?

– Okay, thanks.

Upstairs I sit on a bed (check under it twice) then put my hands on my knees and don't move or touch a thing until they call me down for tea. It is such a weird feeling to walk downstairs and sit and have tea at a table with total strangers you have to live with now.

They talk, they joke.

I am here.

The dad is the boss. That is clear. One foster sister eats like a stick insect, she has plump lips (I'm jealous cos mine are thin and rubbish) and she is skinny and blonde with a light tan from some holiday. The slightly older sister has Marilyn Monroe hair but more nineties style, darker blonde/brunette with a wave and she is super pretty.

After tea the Monroe sister shows me a pack of cigarettes.

– Do you like Minnie?

– The girl I'm to share a room with?

– Aye.

– I don't know.

– She keeps getting caught flashing her arse at the cars when they stop at the traffic lights.

– Okay ...

– It's all a bit fucked up, she goes to see her dad as well because the social worker says it is good for her but you know he ...

The Monroe sister gestures and I feel queasy. I don't know why any social worker would think it was good for her to visit someone who had done that.

– Do you smoke weed?

– Aye, well, I tried it when I was nine!

– I've got some hash for later. What age are you?

– Twelve.

– I hang about with the casuals, in the park, we should go out later to the baked-tattie shop, lots of us hang around there.

– Okay!

I go back to my new room to unpack. The foster mum comes in and picks items from my clothes and she looks visibly dismayed as she turns things over and begins to drop them on the floor into a pile.

– Jenni, you have literally – nothing! You can't wear any of this. It's awful!

She holds up a pair of dark blue cords that were cut off above the ankle and have threads hanging off them; another half a dozen old-fashioned blouses and a few jumpers are lobbed onto the floor as well.

This is an embarrassing moment.

– It's okay, we can apply for a full clothing grant, we will get you everything from scratch, okay? You need the whole lot, pyjamas, school stuff, jeans, I mean – you literally need to throw every single piece of this out.

She looks really sorry for me and a wee bit furious.

– Thank you.

– Another thing I've noticed, Jenni …

– Aye?

– You flinch when someone talks loudly, I am not going to hit you, or shout.

– Okay.

– Also, you swallow rather than cough, you won't even cough in front of people, I just want to say – you can make a noise here.

I so want to disappear into a hole.

Never could cough in front of anyone, hold my breath when I cross a room.

Later on I go to bed and I can smell the carpet freshener.

Sleep is unlikely.

It's better to just think of stuff like there is a little film in my head instead. Like when I got a My Little Pony stable, or Flower Fairies, or how a Girl's World had a knob on her neck so you could just turn it and make her hair grow and how I wanted one of those on my neck because my hair never has grown properly, or how I am going to miss my best friend, or what I did to everyone else when I took the overdose, what it was like when I was in the hospital and how I can never go back to the caravan park again and how nobody from my old life knows what to say to me anyway.

What the fuck am I doing?

In this house.

With these people.

40

We stop at a wall where the market comes once a week. Monroe pulls out a stone. There is a wee gap where she stashes her cigarettes and lighter.

– Don't tell anyone about this spot. I keep my gear here sometimes too.

– Cool.

Light the cigarette and inhale and blow it out in a little thin line and we grin at each other.

– Double drag it, Jenni, we're both late fir school!

It's a dizzy feeling then as we stamp on the butt and she sashays off to school looking like a model and I stand in borrowed clothes at a bus stop. It will be one bus to the village I used to live in, then another one to school. Rattle change and look for the bus coming.

It's my first time back at school since the overdose.

There have been messages sent.

Rumours are going around probably; I don't know what anyone heard.

I don't care.

The bus takes ages. I sit up the back and smoke. The feeling is soothing. Lighter, flare, flame, burnt smell, inhale, smoke, exhale. Look out the window. Think about how I've never really been touched in my entire life. Is that weird? There was not much hugging at my adopted parents' place, not that I would have liked that anyway. I've only had one kiss with a boy really and not like tongues or anything; it was nice though.

Some boys are really funny. They can be super sweet as well. Get off the bus and step into a river of uniforms all flowing into our school, a big red-brick building that looks like a biscuit factory. All the older girls wear the shortest, tightest Lycra skirts, just under their knicker line, and thick black tights, slip-on shoes, soft-soled or Wallabees, or Kickers, white shirts and curly hair, or twisted up so there is a little bump at the front where the fringe is and pinned down with a kirby grip, or long straight blonde hair, and then there are the misfits and the unkempt and boys who cover their jotters in skins from rabbits they hunted, or one who has a ferret he sneaks in down his trousers. I see a guy a few years above me who sucked some other guy's dick in the vennel and everyone slagged them off for being poofs and I felt ashamed of myself for not saying I fancy girls as well. I said it was fine for anyone to date anyone but I didn't say that I would date anyone. I don't know how to tell anyone yet. The classroom is quiet when I go in and the girl who was heading a wee bullying campaign towards me just before I left is sitting on a desk waiting.

– You look so different, Jenni!

– Do I?

– Aye.

– I moved away.

– Aye, look at your hair and yer clothes, wow, you look so different. We heard ay what happened and I just wanted to say that I am totally so glad you are back!

– What did you hear?

– Someone phoned your mum in the caravan and she said, you know, that you … I'm just really glad you're back at school now.

Other kids file in.

I slide behind my desk and look over at her.

– No, you're not.

– What? I am, Jenni!

I catch something in the final notes of her voice.

Fear.

I like it.

– No, you're fucking not glad I'm back, you just wanted to bully me with no fucking comeback and you don't fucking like me at all, and you never did, so do me a favour …

– What?

– Fuck off!

That line was always there.

It's such a useful one.

I am not the same girl that left here weeks ago.

I've been to the other side and walked out the fire and I didn't come back here to take shit from anyone ever again. Mr Mc Arn hands out our assignments that we gave in ages ago.

Short stories.

Everyone gets theirs back except for me. Wonder if he lost it then realise he's holding it in his hands. Mr Mc Arn looks up expectantly at the class. This is bad. I've just made the most headway that I have ever made in my life – against being picked on for being too clever and having huge tits (I fucking hate them) and being a total swot. I have tasted the sweet blood of fuck you! Now Mr Mc Arn is going to shag it all up for me.

He smooths my story out …

– Can you all be quiet please? I want to read this out to the class. This story is incredibly well written and it really got to me and so I'd like you all to just listen.

He puts his glasses on and looks up. I don't look at him, or anyone. He reads the entire thing slowly, he pauses at certain bits and looks up at the class to see if they are taking it in, and just as I think it is over he holds up his hand …

– I'm going to read this bit again – you don't mind, do you, Jenni?

I shrug and one of the boys leers at me.

– *The stray dog tentatively nosed an old baked bean tin …*

Somewhere there is a world where I will be able to live happily and not get picked on for shining. That is not here. I must take what is left of my shine and dull it, hide it, dim the edges of its sharpness. Dinnae get above yerself! Ye think yer better than everyone? What makes you so special? We don't let people just swan around fucking shining in Scotland! Nae cunt likes a smart bastard! Dinnae stoat around acting like yer the bee's knees! I need to take my foster sister's advice – get stoned and stay stoned.

I will quit school in everything but my body.

I am not getting picked on for being clever again!

Not for shining!

– It is so beautifully written, Jenni …

Mr Mc Arn is actually emotional.

I can't look up.

– It is really – brilliant work. Are you still reading as much?

– Nope.

– I see.

I take my story back off him. File out behind the other kids. When I get down to the cafeteria I drop it in the bin, where it belongs.

41

We are all lying on the floor. Giggling! Hysterical! We are in pyjamas which are long T-shirts really. We're all wearing ankle socks. All three of us are shaking cos we are laughing so much. In the absolute purity of our hilarity we don't hear the foster dad come in and I suppose he must get an eyeful of our arses but we have knickers on! He is fucking raging. He shouts at us. He shouts at his wife. He shouts in the hall at anyone who will listen. His anger is like stale cigarette smoke. You can smell it in every room.

We stop laughing.

The Monroe sister gets really nervous around him. I go back to my bedroom next door. Can feel him seething downstairs. Minnie comes in and drops onto the bottom bunk. She cracks her bony fingers. Wherever she goes there is a high-pitched noise. It gets higher when she has been at her dad's, where she had to go at the weekend, again. I get myself dressed and turn away when I am snapping my bra on.

– Do you have to see him?

– Aye.

– Why?

– He's my dad!

– But what he did ...

– I know.

I don't get it.

I think that Minnie's been acting strange lately. We went to Butlins for a holiday and we went to the kids' disco while the adults were in a big entertainment room drinking cocktails or beers. Monroe had every boy at the teenage disco after her. There was one weird one, older, with a soft voice, who kept saying he was going to run his fingers down her spine and it would really turn her on and did she want to feel it? She went around the back with him. I felt insanely jealous. I know she'll never fancy me but he was a weird-faced fuck and a total sleaze! On the dance floor we danced to the La's 'There She Goes' – it's a beautiful song.

Minnie asks me to skive school with her and we go out with these two guys she knows and it is hot out and one of them has her top off right away. The other one is massaging my shoulder. He asks me to go down into the woods so we can be private. I tell him I won't do anything but I go with him to get away from what Minnie is doing, and we lay down and he is heavy, much taller than me, I am tiny, I have like size three feet and little-kid hands. He is panting and his dick is hard. He tries to get me to touch it but I can feel it through his jeans already.

– No!

– No?

– No, I don't want to do that, I said I didn't and I won't.

– What if we wait, what if we get to know each other more?

I've never been allowed to say no to anything, not a person, not a house, not losing my name, not an area, not a friend, not fate, not a fucking stuffed toy duck – and especially not while being ferried through this place and that place under payment and suspicion.

– Okay, we can get to know each other more then?

We walk back up through the woods and I feel scared. I don't want him to come fucking near me. He's way older, not even at school, he's taller than most men. He has blond hair. I don't like him. I think about being real quiet and just going to sit and read somewhere but nobody seems to do that here.

I go down to the kitchen. Dressed now. Ready for the weekend. My foster dad has calmed down. He is cooking soup in a huge pot for later. A fag hangs out his mouth and the cigarette ash grows longer and longer, all fiery with a grey-white column hanging on the end. He does not remove the cigarette from his mouth even once, he just keeps inhaling and blowing smoke out with it clamped in his lips and the blade flashes and thuds as he cuts carrots until eventually that entire column of ash falls into the boiling soup, and he just stirs it in.

42

Minnie is gone. I came back and the bunks were away. I'm now in a different room with a single bed.

– Where?

– Don't know.

Monroe shrugs.

– Did they send her back to her dad?

– Don't know, don't think so.

– Will she be back?

– No.

The foster mother keeps us girls super busy and if it wasn't for her this house would be horrid. She's allied with him though. First and foremost and most obviously in her head. In my last adoption he was an extension of her. She is an extension of him. I am fed up of all of them. Adults just seem to attach their lives totally and completely to someone else – then warp themselves accordingly.

– We are sneaking out tonight, Jenni …

– Where?

– Park, going to meet the casuals, get drunk, get high!

– How?

– When they go to sleep … . you meet me in the hall, we sneak downstairs with our shoes off, climb the fence … go out all night, get home about an hour before they wake up, I've done it before, we just need to make sure the back gate doesn't rattle!

– Okay.

My heart beats hard.

Monroe is the coolest person I know.

She looks like a pin-up but a modern version with Cupid lips and loose jeans and skinny tops and tits higher than mine will ever be and that smile – truly, I'll do whatever Monroe asks me to do and she knows it too.

43

The social work office is an insipid beige. It always looks the same. I have to go through the main office to an interview room through the back. This social worker has blonde hair and she's a bit fat and not in a good way and she is sort of middle class which sounds posh and I can tell she'd be a whole lot fucking happier if I wore tracksuits. I've never liked sporty clothes of any kind. I don't like sport unless riding a BMX is a sport, or skateboarding which I am shit at but it's so graceful. I had a shell suit once. I didn't like that either. I don't like labelled stuff or any of that shit. Monroe wears all of it but she still looks good. It's just not for me. I like black. I like glitter. I like movie stars from the fifties. I am going to a meeting where I will be hated by at least one person. I didn't want to come. The social work department like their protocols so 'adoptive family liaison meet' means I've been having meetings where my adopted mother gets the opportunity to hate me to my face. My adopted dad never says a thing unless it is to agree with her. Dread in every step. I walk with one foot carefully placed in front of the other. They put me in a small interview room to wait. A different social worker comes down to look at me. They all know who I am in here. She is the one from my first adoptive family. I have been asking if I could see her …

I think about that all the time lately.

The big house.

She looks incredibly uncomfortable to see me here looking grown up, and when I catch the expression on her face I'd swear on all the dead grandmothers' graves that she knew at least some of what happened to me in that first adoption.

– So nice to see you, Jenni.

– You too …

– It's been so long though. I heard that you maybe wanted to ask me some questions about the time when I worked with you and I really do wish I could help but I really just can't remember much about back then!

A smile drops from her face, onto the floor, where it squelches away like a slug.

– Okay, then.

I can't catch my breath.

Flashes.

A large rockery and a little girl running around it being called by a new name. A stair. A room. A bowl. A tin opener.

– Okay, it was wonderful to see you, good luck, bye, oh hello, yes, she is in here …

My adopted mother and dad both come in and sit across from me.

The old social worker disappears and I can't think because my adopted mother's face is pursing up as her bespectacled eyes take in my new clothes and my earrings and it is excruciating for her – that I am out of her circle of control.

– So, here we all are then, let's begin today's family meeting … would anyone like tea?

– Yes.

– Milk, sugar, a biscuit?

– Thanks.

I don't accept anything. My own slightly raised chin is a deadly insult. Who the fuck do I think I am? Do I think I can just sit here and get away with this kind of thing? My adopted mother believes herself to be a great victim of my horrid ingratitude.

It is never her that is faulty.

It is always me.

It will always be me.

Oxygen leaves the room. Don't fucking blame it. My blood feels weak. The social worker says things. The adopted husband says one or two things. He isn't my dad. He is her husband and wholly under her spell even though I thought she used to talk to him like a piece of shit. It's not any more okay for a woman to do that than it is a man. I never want to be like her. He doesn't see me. He sees her disappointment. He sees her great charitable act – in taking a child like me. He never saw the way she hit me or pushed at me from morning to night, how I was there to soak up all her anger and work for her, that was my job to work – why get a child like me if we aren't there to do the things nobody else wants to do?

She is so pissed off (fucking raging) I'm not wearing the cheapest least-well-fitted clothes or the doll look, or the Princess Diana one, and I no longer wince whenever her voice is raised. I am not saying I'm not still terrified of the woman – she is glaring and the social worker clears her throat and the adopted dad is just as passive as he ever was. I look at my feet. I want to leave. I am still scared of her and I wish I wasn't but I am. More than anyone else in the world and I always was, she made sure of it from day one. I do not want to be in this room. I feel the hiss of her hatred like a brand on my skin.

– What I can see is that Jenni is getting her hair permed, and wearing – what is that? – tinted lip balm, and those clothes, just to spite me, she is doing this just to get at me!

He nods.

Affirming.

Certain of her like he always was and will be, there was only ever two of them in that family.

There is the social worker.

And me.

– So, how do you feel about that, Jenni? Would you like to respond maybe?

– That's not why I look different.

She glares at me like she really wants to hit me and call me a fucking liar.

– Why did you change your appearance then?

– I want to look like other kids my age.

There is a vibration on the air.

Hot.

Little worms all yellow and red.

They mark things on files. Other things are said. I have done the unthinkable. I have sought to be me.

After they go the social worker finishes writing something down about me, and looks up with a bit of a smile like she feels sorry for me.

– How do you think it went then, Jenni? This is the final family meeting, right?

– I don't want to see them again.

– No.

The social worker doesn't ask it as a question, she just repeats it. We go back out and walk down corridors and emerge onto reception where other little kids are coming in for meetings with parents, or carers, or social workers, and I feel a moment of helplessness for them and me and I keep glancing behind me. I want to see that old social worker's face again. I want to ask her – why she put me in that family?

– Your old social worker is so busy – but she did say to wish you all the very best with your future.

There is a full stop at the end of that sentence.

I am being told not to make contact again.

She's hoping I don't remember.

I do though.

At the back of my throat – I feel my voice begin to go …

Can't speak.

I am in a dark hall, in front of a door – looking into a room with no light.

When you lie in the dark like that night after night!

It's just a black space.

You float.

Terrified.

In the morning when you return to your body – it is always a surprise. I remember her kitchen. The mixing bowl. The attic. I remember it all because I never forgot in the first place.

– Come on, Jenni, get into the car, you are in such a daydream!

When I sit in a social worker's car I can see over the windscreen now, and the road in front and behind – it just runs and runs and runs.

44

Inhale the sweet dark earthy taste of hash. Pop smoke rings like a wizard's child. I am so grateful for hash. It makes me feel happy. I feel – good! And I am – funny! I have a high tolerance. I rarely whitey, I've never been sick on it. It suits me. It is saving me. We are in our long summer of eternal sunshine and warm nights and sneaking out. Life has never been so kind. I have this feeling around the fringes of my mind. It's like freedom. I went to the park last night with Monroe and we drank Peach Concorde and got really drunk and fell down the hill. She is always trying to impress the casuals. She wants to be the coolest girl among them. I don't think she has to try that hard. She is stunning and funny and ultra chic. There are a lot of stylish girls among the casuals in this town. They keep themselves immaculate. Like they just stepped out of *Vogue*. They don't dress like the guys so much. They dress up more. Or if it is lo-fi it's dungarees and tight Lycra tops and their hair cut really nice and their skin is flawless and they wear expensive chunky trainers and fine gold chains and they always have perfect lipstick on. There are two red-haired sisters who are really fashionable but in a unique way, like they learned how to dress in New York. One has a short bob cut that is super shiny and she wears bright catsuits and platform shoes and her sister has long red hair all the way down her back in curls and they are both super slender and they saw a dead person and told me about it, some old guy on their street, they saw his corpse and I wanted to see it too because it seems like all I want to do is study humans, even if they are not breathing. I'm nowhere near as cool as anyone. It's okay though. Something is lifting in me. Even if I have to get high to learn what it is like to feel happy, I am grateful cos I never thought I'd have this chance, to just step out and listen to music, and hang out with teenagers in the park all night while the adults are asleep. This is the best summer of my life.

I so wanted to be cool like the other kids.

45

Monroe flirts with everyone. All the boys say we have come-to-bed eyes. They are all so much older than me.

– You have to go with him if he wants to go for a walk with you, he's cool, it will make you look good!

– Okay, Monroe, I will, steady!

– And you need to sneak out and go to the Kronk too.

– Why?

– It ups our cool if you are seen in the right places and you need to get really high when you do go, you need to take E and some speed, I'll get you the money.

– Where are you getting all the cash from?

– My aunt has money all over her house! Honestly, I put my hand down her couch and there is so much money there, she never notices!

We are walking through fields because I want to go and look for the old house I used to live in with the first adoptive family. If I can find it I feel like I will be able to articulate something really important. It can't be that far from here because the ballet school I went to as a tiny wee girl is in the town hall. It is right by the Toll where the casuals hang out all day and night, on Toll Patrol. That means if another town's casuals come through, they'll get battered by our ones – it goes back decades among older gangs that fought each other, and there used to be black calling cards left and if you got one you were dead. I don't pay much attention really. Casual clothes and all that stuff isn't for me. I am more alternative, or something! I do love to be high though. We walk through grassy fields and it is so sunny. I inhale the joint as deep as I can and sing and we laugh and feel the heat of summer on our skin. It's been better since we got back from Spain. My foster parents made me go for swimming lessons before we went cos I didn't know how to swim and then diving lessons where I belly-flopped into the pool in front of everyone every week while my foster sister walked onto the diving board as neat as a gymnast (she is) and did a perfect Round Dolph flip and dive each time. The foster parents didn't want me to embarrass them in Benidorm but I definitely would if I dived. I can't dive worth a fuck. I've only just learned to swim! When we were away I fell asleep on my lilo and got third-degree burns all over my face and because I am normally so pale it's not even funny. They had to cover me in natural yogurt to cool the red burns. I lay there hallucinating for days. My foster dad shouted – we take you on holiday and this is how you fucking repay us? Then I had a fight with Monroe. She tried to batter my head off the radiators when the foster parents were out. We made up but I trust her less than I did before. Then we came home and forgot about it. On the way back to my foster parents we go to visit Monroe's pal who gets us weed. They got me to skin up on her ironing board for days until each joint I roll is so perfect it could win competitions. Spliff-rolling is an art. The girl has an attic bedroom. It's massive and one entire gable-end wall is just a display of a thousand stacked-up empty Marlboro Lights boxes. Monroe made me pretend to be tripping last week and we've been sneaking out the house most nights but tonight I am stay-ing with a girl who I've met a few times and who seems nice.

– What time are you going to meet him then, Jenni?

– I don't know. What age is he?

– I don't know. Anyway, tell me which guy you think I should go for, you said you'd think about it and you are good at knowing what is the right thing to do and I need to decide.

She looks at me with one green eye and the other blue-grey.

– If you go for the super good-looking one who everyone wants to go out with you will fall in love with him and have a great time but he will always be the equivalent of a prick-tease, he's always going to want attention from the other girls, he won't give that up. You'll always think he's going to cheat on you and he'll always be searching for the best-looking girls to flirt with, basically, it won't be real. However, if you go out with the other one, he gets a lot more respect from everybody and he's going to actually adore you, go with him if you really want to feel loved.

– How'd you get so clever?

– I'm not.

– You fucking are! My parents say how smart you are, you're grade A in everything and you don't even try. Right, go to your pal's to stay but come to the park and I'll give you speed and E's and then you can go for a walk with the guy, everyone thinks he's cool as fuck, it'll be good for your reputation!

What she is not saying is that I am so uncool that I'm lucky he wants to talk to me at all. I go to Dana's. She is not right in the head. She fights with her mum. Her mum is pissed off but she is nice enough. She is out when I get there. We roll joints and put on a horror film. It's called *Nightmare on Elm Street*. Even though it is only the afternoon it is super creepy. We sing the song about 1, 2 and Freddy coming for you … and her house seems really empty and then her mum comes back and

asks me if Dana has told me about how she tried to steal her
car and how she needs to be good.

– Fuck all this, we are going out!

– Dana, be back by eleven?

– Aye, whatever, aye.

It always blows my mind when girls talk to their mums like
that. Their mums must really like them to let them away with
it. It's such a nice sunny evening but it's getting darker by
the time we go to the park. There's casuals everywhere. We
are so stoned already. They sit in groups of tens, twenties.
There must be about fifty casuals in one bit of the park at least.
Everyone dresses so smart; even if I personally don't like a
two-stripe Adidas top, the boys look good, elegant in their
way, young and fit and at their most beautiful, some guys look
like models. Every girl has perfect make-up and smokes and is
funny. A car flies in and Monroe pulls down her window. She
is high as fuck.

– Come here!

– What?

– Here's some speed, take that, go on, and an E, take it in
front of me so I see!

– Okay!

– Look, he's over there, go ...

I say bye to Dana for now and then go over to the edge of
the park where the guy is – like he doesn't want anyone to see
us leave. It is proper dark out now. Stars sparkle. The air is
cold. I don't know where we are walking. Up through the
estate. Down streets. Away out to where the big houses are. I
can feel speed kicking in and the E too, I'm beginning to
shine – that's what drugs do, bring out the bit of me I always
have to hide. Maybe it's why I love them.

46

He takes me up a private bit of road. It looks like it leads to a fancy house but we veer off to an open bit of grass with trees around it and into a clearing which is hidden from view.

– Sit next to me then, Jenni.

– Why?

– Just to talk.

I am shining even brighter than the moon.

My eyes glow.

– Who do you know, Jenni?

– What d'you mean?

– In all the different towns, where you go to school, or here?

– Nobody.

He nods.

– Lie down.

– Why?

– We can look at the stars.

His mouth hot on mine. Tongue. Not sure, try to do it right. On top of me. Wiry hair and dark eyes and he yanks my jeans down.

– Don't!

Wriggle to pull them back up. He has hard fingers like tree branches.

– Just stay still, it's okay.

As he pulls out his thing I try to drag my whole body up the hill away from him and my breath is gone – stars watch cold as they have ever been. He is way heavier than I am and probably twice as old and she said just to come for a walk with him and I was just hoping someone might think I was not … lame.

– Stop! It's going to hurt!

He slams one hand on either shoulder.

Grip like a vice.

Cold blood in my veins, the trees are all waving their arms at me to get away.

My body freezes.

It's like being cut open with thousands of tiny little knives.

I can't tell what sound is any more.

Whose body is this?

I am sure it has little to do with me.

I've left it down there.

Done that before, haven't I? Just left it!

It is not mine. I don't want it. It's just a place I used to live. Don't want to go back to it. Up above there is a sky. It has stars. Thousands and millions of stars made of carbon and gas and dust and they are all – just watching.

47

I am like the frog – always boiling, so much that it doesn't even understand that is what is happening to it. I walk down roads I've never seen before. Windows lit. It is so sore. Look at people living in those cosy rooms with people they know. Yellow lamps glow through windows. Locked doors with names on them. Imagine clean bathrooms that smell of lavender. It's so strange. Their life, then mine, walking streets I don't know, not feeling like there is one place like that, truly, for me. It is so sore to walk. I am trying not to cry. Not to sit down and sleep here on the pavement. I force myself to keep walking. Just keep looking straight ahead. I will recognise something soon.

48

Tap lightly on Dana's window.

– Are you okay?

– Aye.

She lets me in. Try to sit down on her beanbag in between her teddies and her Lycra tops.

There is a night light in the shape of a moon.

We both lie down in the dark and she says things and I make answers back of some kind. After a while she falls asleep. I don't. I check under her bed for her. She's okay. Shadows on the walls put on a play all night. They are creeping around all night long.

There is a memory of a memory.

I am shrinking.

Someone is pounding along a corridor.

I am tiny.

Sit awake all night. Arms clasped around my knees. The birds wake eventually. A sinister aria goes out across the town. My eyes are bleary with grit. I bet I smell. In my pants. I want to scream and cry and bathe. This is not my house though. There is not a door on this entire earth that I could walk through and say was home.

49

Monroe is putting on lip gloss – perfect as ever.

– What the fuck happened?

– Nothing.

– I don't believe you …

– He did it. So!

– What?

– The whole thing, he *did* it.

– You – shouldn't have let him do that!

She is so mad at me, hand on hip, short blonde wavy hair and her perfect figure and her nice house and parents (adopted or not) that she has always lived with since a baby and she's acting like I did something wrong when she was the one who said I should hang out with him and I want to cry and it still hurts to sit and I hate every single atom of my life!

– I said I didn't want to …

– What?

– I …

She looks at me for a long hard minute.

Narrows her eyes.

Checks herself out in the mirror and she is really, really angry now.

– Do you want people to think you're a slag? You're only twelve years old!! You need to fucking sort yourself out, Jenni!

A hot slick of shame all over me.

She will be in the park with the casuals (including the guy from last night) and everyone wants to hang out with anyone who makes them seem cool and they couldn't give a fuck what happens to a girl like me. They never will.

I am nothing.

Take my clothes off. Place them in a bin. Go into the bathroom and turn the shower on hot.

What will I do if I'm pregnant?

50

Scuff feet. Push back on swing. I used to love to go higher and higher and lean up to look at the sky. I don't want to think a certain thing. It has gone around in my head for days. I don't want to think about how I said no. What it meant, what it should mean, that I said no. My feet are still so tiny. Just there at the end of my legs.

I don't want to go to school tomorrow.

51

The trees grow taller. Nobody could climb them. The forest floor is mulched and sodden and the leaves are slimy and trodden by hundreds of kids running down through here on the way to school every morning. A muddy river whorls slowly at the bottom of the slope. There's always someone falling in. Or losing their bag. Or smoking, hidden by big tree trunks. The teachers hide behind them sometimes to catch us. There is a chase then. Right in the middle of the woods there is an empty stone swimming pool. Nobody knows why it is there. It has never been warm enough to have an outdoor swimming pool in this country. Every year when summer is over it fills with leaves.

I was bleeding. A lot. Big clots.

Then it stopped.

52

I have half an hour when I get back before anyone else will be in. I take out a packed bag that I hid under the stairs this morning behind my paper-run stuff. I put a few more things in it. Sing the song to myself about the blackbird. It sings in the dead of night. Take my bag and walk out the door.

Close it behind me.

53

Crescent moon. Tiny luminous nail. Far up there. Huge hulking bridge on knobbly elbows. Like a flying monkey from Oz. It looks like the bridge could just creak upright and walk out of here. Don't look behind me. Lots of things watch a girl who lives in a forest. Especially at this time of night. Everyone is gone.

It is nearly three in the morning.

Tuck my feet under my hooded top.

I am a strange owl.

My hood is pulled right up so only my eyes peek out.

There's a lot of tree spirits so I have to be still. I am sitting on a plastic bag. The ground is cold and wet. There are loads of huge spiders. They are hungry. Me too. We are forest dwellers, me and the arachnids. I have one spare T-shirt, seventeen cigarettes and weed. I don't turn around. The forest people are stood next to each of the trees just staring at me.

Night growls with little animals and the wind and things under the earth ripple and raise themselves up. The hard red eye of my cigarette looks out for me. It begins to rain. I double, triple inhale.

54

I don't know how Monroe found me but she did.

– Do you need anything?

– Pants, socks, and a blanket.

– I've money and weed here – I'll come back in a few days, okay?

– Aye.

Watch as she disappears.

It is my third morning out here.

My face is in the paper.

Have to be careful not to be seen.

I do each day like this; spend the night as a silent creature of the forest. Stay terrified. Wait for dawn. Stand up. Stamp my feet. Try to get the cold out of me. It's early September but it is freezing. Walk back roads to a corner newsagent in the nearby village. If cars come – shrink back. The police are looking for me. Buy the same thing each morning. Cream soda. Three packets of 10p pickled onion crisps. A chocolate bar. Cigarettes, skins, matches. Go back to the viaduct and take my clothes off and bathe in the river. Lay down naked on the stones. Minnows dart beneath my feet. Let my hair fan out in the freezing water. Once I'm so cold I'm numb all over I wash my knickers in the current and hang them up to dry. Sit. Smoke. Pull on my T-shirt. The water is running fast. It gurgles over slimy flat river pebbles. A dragonfly hovers over the rapids. It's so gorgeous! Long reeds of water tug gently.

I am hungry.

There is a tiny bit of motion away up on the hillside. Someone! More than one person … the bushes move as they make their way through them and I get my jeans on so fast, heart beats, beats, beats. Four guys crash out of the trees with big grins. One of them says things, like that there is an old paedophile looking for me that everyone knows around here. Need to be safe. There is a caravan they can break into so I can stop sleeping in the woods. I want to never sit alone all night in a forest again. Two nights ago I went to a kid's house party when their parents were away but they wouldn't let me stay and when I walked back to the viaduct in the dark on my own I had never felt quite so cold or alien. Last night the forest people didn't hide behind the trees. They just stood in a circle around me.

– Okay.

– Cool, I'll see you there at seven and you can't make a noise cos the security guy has a massive dug that he sets on anyone who he finds breaking in there.

– Aye.

That makes me feel sort of safer.

They go home to houses with heaters and fridges and doors.

All that's not for me. Leaves poke through my shoulder blades, my teeth have silver river fish dashing between them and the moon knows I am its only child because I am made entirely of bone.

55

I am so thin now my bones stick out at my hips. We duck under barbed wire. A large V of geese flies high up in the last minutes of blue sky. The oldest guy from the group, I think he is in his twenties somewhere but I can't tell, he opens a locked caravan door with a wee chib. We slip into the dim. I can't see his face. So hungry I can't think straight. The caravan is damp but it doesn't let the wind in at least and there are bound to be some blankets. The forest people will have to walk a way to find me here.

He lights a cigarette and so do I.

– Lie on the floor.

The windows of the caravan have round corners with rubber on them. I know that because I grew up in a caravan park. I also know this isn't a question. I am to do it quickly, or it will be worse. I just need to not think about the breath going from me. Or the smell of damp carpet. Him pushing me down. I just think instead about how the last minutes of blue in the sky are always the most beautiful each day, that I must look for the light just half between sky and some other world, where I am not left lying on a floor, in pain, and so cold, but beyond hunger, I am leaving my body again.

56

One day some happy family will be sat here having their tea who don't know that ages ago a skinny twelve-year-old had been lying where they walked to and fro on their holidays. They will cook boiled eggs and toast and play cards while it rains outside and they will fight, but later tell stories in the dark, and I think about them having a nice holiday one day, and they will be walking right over this spot on the floor where I can smell only damp and the disgusting cold horror of a man standing to pull up his zip.

It is better when he is gone.

Try to clean myself.

There is a smell where he stuck himself inside me.

My eyes adjust to darkness. I find a yellow terry-towel-type thin blanket like my granny used to have on top of the bed. It has sort of lines down it where the pattern is raised. There is a jaggy blanket too but it is thicker. This caravan stinks. I am alive. I can feel my bones, my breath. I did not make it through my overdose to not know what it means to still be alive. It means I must survive everything. Force myself to breathe deeply. Pull the blanket around me. My mother the moon is looking for me. The forest people tell her I have gone from the woods so she retreats behind clouds in some kind of mourning. There will be no light out tonight. I sit totally still. I am listening to everything. Call of an owl. Grass rustling out there as the wind combs its way across the fields. Ants will be marching. The man goes around with his torch – it blares up

on the wall of the caravan for a minute like a white eye –
looking, his dog sniffs at the steps.

I don't sleep.

Sneak out early. Shop. Fields. Bridge. River to bathe in the
cold, cold water until I am almost clean.

57

Caravan door firmly closed. The light is kind of orange yellow. The whole caravan moves on its haunches in the wind. Might die in here. Draw lipstick pictographs on the wall just in case. A hangman with the letters of my name on it. A house with a little path and eyes for windows. A peace sign and an ohm, some kind of spell. He has been here the last three nights on his own. Tonight he opens the door and four more guys file in behind him.

Heart drops.

No.

I have no money left and no cigarettes and no food. I've been drinking water out the river. I feel weak. Sick. Everything is hazy. They sit in a row making wee jokes to each other. Fear in my gut. Sit in the half-light. Can't reach the door. I am so thin by now living out here like a strange mushroom who never really had the moon for a mother.

– What age urr ye?

– Twelve.

– Fuck's sake!

They snort like something is really, really fucking funny.

They are laughing *at* me.

I'm a thing.

– You lot sit there …

He orders them around – they are all on the seating at one end of the caravan. They are only one step away from the bed platform he is pulling out. I can't reach the door. Smell of alcohol. He pushes me onto the platform bed.

Holds his hand up to his lips …

– Ssssssshhhhh.

Pat-a-pat-pat-pat-rrrrrrrrrrrrr-ddt.

How much does it take before a heart stops?

One of the guys is muttering that I better not piss him off and he drags at my clothes so they can see and they are all watching.

– I don't want to.

– Lay down.

– No!

– Shut the fuck up!

– I'm scared …

I whisper that bit …

He directs a laugh towards the guys, this is his performance, and I am not getting my lines right. He shoves my body into the shapes that he wants. I am colder than the river now. Older than my mother moon. I am angrier than the sea. As he does it he talks to them, and makes comments, and slaps me and turns me and I think they touch themselves too and they all watch and watch and watch.

58

One of the other ones tried to come back in to do it and I argued like I was the devil himself. I said I was the guy who did it's girlfriend. I said that the sky would fall, that I'd kill everyone he knew, that I'd die of crying – I told him to wait and come back tomorrow – I said literally anything to close the door.

Wrapped in a horrid blanket.

Sit awake all night, jumping at any sound.

Wait to see the torch when the security man does his rounds.

The sun will be here far too late, I will be gone, soon as the moon stops falling.

59

Rub my body red raw in the river. Step out of the rapids. Begin to retch. I vomit over and over and over again. I can't stop! I have one dry T-shirt and some dirty jeans. Haul them on. Go the front roads only stopping to be sick. Doesn't matter if the police see me now. Go to my best friend's dad's caravan. He will drive me to hand myself in. I will say nothing. There will be a world that will move outside the window. His vehicle will smell like a part of my childhood. I will watch my voice go away up in the sky far beyond any kite and just … let it go.

60

It's a secure unit for young offenders. The furniture is nailed to the floor so nobody can throw it at the staff. All the doors get locked at night. I get a hot cup of tea. Staff talk to each other in stressed tones.

– We are so sorry but there are no rooms in the unit tonight.

– Okay.

– We are trying really hard to find you a place.

– Thanks.

My friend's dad says goodbye and I go to the bathroom and look at myself.

Old child, I used to think I was so tall, but I stopped growing.

They won't let me bath yet. I want to lie down on the floor. I want to cry my heart out but I can't let anyone know or what would those guys do if they found me again? What feels like hours later they come back into the office where I've been waiting.

– So sorry! Okay, we have finally found I think the only place that will take you tonight. It is a battered women's refuge, it really is the only place we can send you, Jenni, it's usually for grown-ups but it will do for a few days, okay? You might be there a week tops, we really need to find a children's unit that has a place free for you to go to after that.

– Okay.

I am driven to the battered women's hostel on one of the roughest council estates miles away.

Admitted.

Filed.

Stamped.

The police come out and charge me for absconding and they are angry and annoyed and do I know that I have wasted police time and resources and do I know how much it costs the tax-payer when children like me go missing and I don't bother to tell them about the other time I got picked up for running away (once before this) where one of their men told me if his partner hadn't been there he'd have kicked my fucking cunt in.

I don't say that.

After they charge me I am allowed to go and sit in the living room.

The only other resident in here is a schizophrenic guy who headbutts the walls all night.

He sees me in the hall and stares at me in silence.

Why is a guy in here anyway?

Then my foster parents come to tell me they don't want me to come back because I have absconded and obviously become an issue and they have other children to think about but they bring me some clothes and that's the last I see of them. A lovely member of staff who looks absolutely fucking knackered calls me into the wee office.

– You've been here all day, Jenni, and you didn't tell anyone?

– What?

– It is your thirteenth birthday today! Did you forget?

– No.

I feel really dumb.

– This isn't much, sweetheart, but … here's a new packet of twenty cigarettes, from me to you, and there is a tub of ice cream in the kitchen freezer, please help yourself, I think there's some fizzy juice in there too, and there is a really good Kylie Minogue video in the communal room. You can watch it as many times as you want, okay? Tomorrow they are going to blow up the high-rises on the hill so maybe you can watch from the garden?

– I'd like that, thank you.

I don't want to cry.

So.

I don't.

That sweetheart though, that gentle word.

Hold it to me like a teddy.

Later on my adopted mother phones the battered women's refuge to say that she hopes I am having a really, really great birthday.

She is such a sarcastic bitch.

I bet this has made her really fucking happy.

61

They lay all the explosives carefully on the middle floors. Someone gets to press the button. Wish it was me! They blow the high-rise flats up! It's the best thing I've ever seen that wasn't on TV. Huge billows of smoke curl high up into the sky as windows and walls fold in towards each other. The block of high-rise flats drops neatly to the ground like a building on its knees, then the last bit goes too. They do it to a few buildings one after another in a row. I stand in the garden (a bit of concrete) outside the battered women's hostel and smoke cigarettes and think about how one day I will blow something up – I want to do that so fucking badly.

62

This kitchen smells different to the last house. There is always
something. Tea drinkers vs coffee, wine or lager, or boiled rice,
veggie pasta, or fry-ups or herbs, or different washing-up liquid,
or those who clean vs those who don't, and for a while I smell
a bit like whatever house I am in as if there is no smell that
actually belongs to me other than the White Musk oil I buy in
tiny bottles for four quid at the Body Shop, or that brief phase
where I tried wearing hairspray but I fucking hated it. Insette
hairspray is the most flammable substance on earth. I use
Insette to make flame-throwers now. Spark a lighter and then
spray – it gives off a hell of a flame. Some of the people I live
with are quiet. Others are not. Some are a tiny bit posher – like
this one, who lives in a cottage with a fireplace and wears trousers made of things like hemp. She burns incense. There are
pretty flowers in the garden. If I was to live somewhere I was
able to choose when I was older (as if) it would be like this cottage. It is a dark low-ceilinged space with a dense and heavy
silence and a bookcase and a wood stove. We talk very quietly
to each other in the kitchen because her husband is upstairs
riddled with cancer.

    – You'll only be here a few weeks.

    – I know. I will sleep in the attic and I promise I will stay
totally out of your way.

    – He is getting treatment this week, we can't have any noise.

    – Of course!

    – Thank you.

I feel very protective of the woman in this cottage with her husband who is trying not to die and I am the last person who is going to give either of them any hassle. I wipe the counters when she is upstairs. Put things in the bin. Make sure when I go to the loo I take my toothbrush and toothpaste back out so it's like I am not even here. There is a feel of death all over the milk in the fridge and also in the bath and in the hall and in the kitchen, and when I touch the burning kettle which has just boiled, where she has taken him tea, I can feel it on the scalding metal and in the chipped ceramic mug that I sit and sip in her kitchen. I sit at that worn kitchen table and think about when I move from here – which will be as soon as she can get rid of me (I don't disrespect it – being with someone dying is a whole job). I have decided that I will learn to cope with what has happened in my life by never going back – to any place I lived before. Then I can forget the things that happened there. The me I was in the place before is gone. I can become someone else, a new me.

There is a guitar in the living room.

Don't touch it.

Hum to myself real low, don't see that she is walking by in the corridor.

– You have a beautiful voice, Jenni.

– Thank you.

– It's okay to make a little noise, just not upstairs.

The woman wants to know about the casuals up in town. Some guy from this town had his trainers taxed in the village next door and then he was sent back here barefoot so they are all fighting again. They have been stealing clothes off washing lines too, even frozen ones, walking them off like designer cardboard cut-outs with flat invisible humans in them. There is a girl who lives down the hill, who told me a guy wanted to do a rainbow kiss with her, like if she had not swallowed and he went down on her then they French-kiss and mix blood and sperm together. Better not write about that on my next English assignment, if I ever make it back to school. It sounds utterly gross. She told me about the Mars bar game too, when a guy puts a Mars bar inside a girl then tries to eat it out. I don't want anyone's mouth fucking near me and the only French thing I want to do is smoke well and drink coffee. I sit in front of the woman's little fire and blow smoke rings. One after another until a whole row of them hover in the air. If you really practise you can blow a small smoke ring through a bigger one. There is nothing more satisfying. It's all in how you click your jaw. I once blew seventeen smoke rings in a row and twice now I have blown three smoke rings right through each other and if that doesn't make me a fucking prophet then nothing ever will.

I drink coffee all the time now.

Smoke endlessly.

Every morning I draw out the same hangman I drew in lipstick on the caravan wall. Neat little dashes underneath it. - - - - - - - - - just enough to spell out my name.

63

There are so many things they don't ask. Social workers or foster parents, teachers, police, doctors, friends' parents, everyone that knows me. Nobody has ever asked – what happened to you? What are we not getting right? What don't we know? What can we do for you? Who are you? What do you miss? Who hurt you? What can we do to get them? I don't get asked those questions. They are scared of what I might answer.

Or maybe they want to make sure they don't have to do something about it?

What I try not to think about – after I leave the cottage – is how both times I said no.

It makes me panic.

I said, no.

What does it mean? Really? My adopted mum never let me say no to anything. Don't answer back. Be polite. Warp whatever is in you so others feel fine. It is like, I must have no feelings that could alarm. No eyes. No voice, no teeth, no claws, no sinew, no marrow, no knees, no ankles, no wrists. No wants. I have no stomach. I have no heart. I have no dreams. I have no talent. I have no hope. I have no fist. I have no body. I have no soul, I have no heart, I have no memory. I have no future. There is a singer I love called Nina Simone who says this all so much better than anybody ever will because she is a fucking genius but that doesn't mean this life didn't fell her many times too and when I hear one of her songs it does something to me that I can't explain yet.

64

They are going to cut out my brain. It would be exceptionally helpful if they did. It's no use to me. It never stops thinking. It is fucking incessant. I don't know what its issue is. It wants to know everything about the world and humans and stuff and I am tired by its endless searching. It tells me I'm bad all the time too.

– Undress behind the curtain, please, Jenni.

I pull it around me, little jangly silver hoops make a cheery wee song.

– Do I need to have a full medical every time I move?

– Yes, turn around, Jenni.

I rotate all white-and-blue-skinned.

Furless rat.

Since I got back from sleeping rough I am thinner than I've ever been, my ribs stick out now but my breasts still won't disappear. I hate them. I always wear clothes that cover them up. I don't wear anything low-cut. Not ever!

I've cut my hair off.

It is short now. I don't wear lipstick. Never did! I don't like the feeling of it on my mouth. I wear a touch of mascara. That's it. I have big eyes and I want to make them bigger so people might notice that I can see everything.

Once the doctor is done I dress methodically.

– Jenni is underweight, considerably more so than before.

This is stated quietly to the social worker. I feel a bit of triumph! I have learned how not to eat. I like to be as numb as I possibly can be. I like to see the sparkle in stars as they begin to fade out. I like to see the orange glow of lamp posts at night. I like flowers. I like pretty things. I like girls but only the ones who are actually nice human beings. I like fashion shows. I still like thinking about New York. Being an artist, or a writer, and living with all my cats in an apartment in New York until I am old, and all my friends would be interesting and we would talk often and go for walks and drink gin instead of tea. Dreaming is vital. There has to be more to my life than days like this. I like dancing. I like singing. I like learning. I like reading. I like baking. I like remembering my days with my best friend where we were safe in her house at weekends and at night she'd say tell me a story – and I'd say give me a subject – and she'd say something random like a three-legged dog – and I'd make her up a whole story on the spot and keep telling her it as she went to sleep. I like it when cars go fast over bumps. I like butterflies in my stomach. I like orderly things in a neat row. I am learning (much of the time) to find ways to dull my sadness. I place a chemical blanket over my anger. It is important. I don't look back. Not ever! When I go from a place I am gone.

– There is something else …

The doctor interrupts my thoughts.

– Yes?

My social worker is mildly pissed off at having to write down even more fucking information and not being able to get out of here before the traffic is busy in town.

– She has completely stopped growing, not even a millimetre in some time, which can happen, but also how are your periods lately, Jenni?

– Well, they're just dandy, doctor – real swell!

He half smiles at that, an adult with an actual sense of humour – someone knock me out!

– When did you first get your period again?

– When I was nine years old!

– I see. And you've always had this thin strip of fuzzy hair down your back?

– One hundred per cent gremlin.

– Is it hormones, doctor, from trauma? I know there are a lot of studies on it now, the social worker adds, seeming interested once more.

– My nails only grow when I take amphetamines, I tell them solemnly.

– Really? she says.

– Aye. Am I like, fucking dead or something?

– Don't swear, please, Jenni, it's hours until I can get a glass of medicinal wine!

The doctor smiles.

– Your hair must be growing! It doesn't grow?

The social worker seems more alarmed at the idea of this than anything else. She really is quite a funny one.

– Not really, or not fast, or at all really. Look, is this it? Can I go? Am I going to be this size forever?

The doctor looks up.

– I think perhaps for various reasons …

– I was one of the tallest kids in my primary school for years, I was one of the two fastest runners all the way through primary school and I once won the 'Robert Burns' prize for singing 'Mull of Kintyre'!

– No? Well done! Really?

The social worker looks like she needs me to go and score her a wee gram of something.

– Good on you, the doctor says.

– I'm not that small, like we used to go and visit two sisters in the last family, they had a flat they shared in supported accommodation and they had all this like low furniture and a tiny kitchen and they were about this big ... like up to my waist maybe but their hands were bigger and they were super-funny women, smart as hell, and they don't like the word midget because it's not even vaguely accurate, they have dwarfism and it doesn't hold them back one fucking bit, so I am sure I will survive with my little-kid hands and feet too, I was on LSD last time I saw the sisters, they'd just had a new kitchen fitted.

The social worker seems like that one will just finish her off nicely before she escapes for the weekend.

The doctor looks at me with a gentle smile.

– I'm the size of a child, doctor?

– You *are* a child, Jenni.

– Will my hands always be this tiny?

I hold them up fingers splayed.

– Quite possibly, and you seem very healthy, although you need to quit smoking and all the other things, quit those too! So, Jenni's had her inoculations and is up to date on vaccines, so that's us!

The nice doctor signs a piece of paper and I am placed back in the hands of the social work department and as we leave it begins to spit outside.

– How far is the new unit?

– It's about an hour's drive from here.

– How will I get to school?

– It will take two buses, half an hour on each one.

– Okay.

– It's important you stay in the same school, Jenni, it is your only continuity.

She opens her boot. Moves one of my bin bags out the way. They are what I move all my stuff in.

– How many kids are in the unit?

– Twelve.

We drive through streets I know and ones I don't and it is all unfamiliarly normal. There is a thing I don't say to her or anyone else. I am nervous. About the other kids in there. What will they be like? Will I have to fight on the first night? I don't want to. I just want to be okay. I don't want anything else horrid to deal with. But there is another fear under that, a knot in my gut that tells me something about my anger, how long it has been there – getting more warped, waiting. It turns out what I'm scared most of – is me.

I'd rather die than hurt someone though. That thought comforts me. I count the white cars as we drive along. So far I've seen sixteen.

65

We go through villages and estates and then up a long road with a huge tall wall and through gates and down a driveway and up to a car park and there is a minibus with SOCIAL WORK DEPARTMENT emblazoned on the side of it. The kids' unit is rectangle and it looks like it was built super cheap and it is surrounded by grass and then there is a big Victorian mansion over a field and then another small house nearer to us.

– That's the little kids' home where the wee ones under nine stay!

– That's mean – why are they not with families?

– Lots of reasons. Over there you can see the disabled children's residential school, it's that big Gothic building through the trees.

– Will I have to share a bedroom?

– I hope not.

She gets out the car and I do too, go up to the front door and ring the bell and an officer in charge admits us and we all have to go through to the office and then there is a meeting and a support worker (some woman) is allocated to me and there are faces and a tour of the children's home, two downstairs toilets, one for boys, one for girls, a smoking room (absolute bonus), the laundry room (cheery woman in there), a living room with some dining tables and a cook (pretty sure he just got out of prison – a wee smile from him) – he's baking chocolate eclairs of all things! Everything is cheap – carpets, chairs, windows – the colours are beige or grey, wee bit of red, there is a room at the back of the unit with a pool table in it and a record player (that is something), then upstairs, two more bathrooms (one for girls, one for boys).

– You must take a bath every night at the same time, it is mandatory.

– Great.

– You will not leave your room after ten o'clock.

– Okay.

We pass a scraggy wee cunt with specs and curly hair and fingers like bone, all fleshy gums, and huge teeth and creepy. I know he is a cunt cos I've been doing this a while now. I am learning. I am shown into a little room with one square window, a chest of drawers, a small wardrobe and a single bed. My bin bags squat on the floor waiting for me.

I am left to unpack alone.

Grateful.

Want to run away.

Already!

A girl pokes her head around my door.

Downstairs I can hear kids coming in from different schools, or in taxis from special schools, and there is noise and clatter and deodorant sprayed and music, and she looks at me with big brown eyes and freckles and a smile.

– Ye want a smoke?

– Aye, I do!

Follow her down into the smoking room where she lights up with a blue haze. I inhale, the fags laced heavily with weed. We smile at each other. I get the warmest feeling from her right away, and other kids I meet that day (not all – some stay back, some are gnarly – but most of them) give this feeling of – kindness, intrigue, openness, they really like me.

It's highly disarming.

There's a threat around the edges at times but mostly not for me. I feel weirdly held and seen and an utter relief – at not living with a stranger's family. There are about eight main members of staff on rotation then some that come in for shifts but who also work in other units as well. One of the strangest things is how they all take notes on me. All day! What I eat, when I sleep, if I get charged, all of it. One of the staff was having sex with one of the girls (apparently), she is blonde and chubby as hell with a podgy nose and a cute smile, and one of the guys is suspect with more than one of the boys, and another member of staff comes into my room later on and tells me with some kind of pink-scrubbed-face glee that it has only just been passed that staff can't strip-search me on sight any more.

– Okay.

– Aye, the legislation has just come in.

– Right.

The officer in charge comes on later and she is a harassed woman and definitely a stoner. Then there is a worker with bobbed dark hair. Her husband is a policeman down in the village and everyone (kids) has to bathe within certain hours and dinner is in the dining space and I get used to the entire routine within about three days flat.

– Someone's been in Creep's room with a knife, a wee boy says.

– Who has been in there?

Shrug.

– Why?

– Wee cunt raped a dog, that's what they're saying, broke its legs after, got caught – his parents keep coming to visit him and they give him money and he catches trains and goes on these mad train rides, all day, all week.

– Where's he going?

– Fuck knows.

I exhale. Thought he was a cunt first time I saw him. Everything you need to know in a unit is found out in the smoking room, or after lights out when we quietly open our windows their six allocated inches (so we can't jump from them) to swing lit fags or joints along to each other on shoelaces and talk and giggle and then close the windows later on and climb into bed and this is the good bit – there is nobody to disappoint and I'm not mistrusted on sight here, not by any of the other kids, and it feels like in residential, for a wee while at least, I've found a place I actually want to be.

66

I'm barefoot in jeans standing with my arms up above my head – behind Scotmid. The air is cold. I am stoned immaculate. I am high like a wild thing. Savage like sin. Wasted to the hilt. I am stoned like moon bait. I'm a cavewoman. I am scratching out drawings of human history on stone. I get stoned like I mean it. I am not fucking around. I'm taller when I'm stoned. I am a rabbit. I am gentle. I am young again. I get stoned because it makes me feel beautiful.

– Hurry up, Jenni.

– What?

The problem with straight people is they are not stoned. Her uniform is blue. Or, maybe it is black? Is it black? Can't tell. Think it is. My T-shirt is white. It is tight. It is really fucking Baltic out. I haul it over my head and hold it out like there might be a laundry basket near the bins at the back of fucking Scotmid or something.

– Spread your legs.

– Fuck off.

– What did you say?

The policewoman is literally raging. I'm just off the Main Street in the village. Sneakers on their side. There is a hole in one sock. I don't yet know how long it will be until I can go up into the woods and roll a big fat joint. The policewoman gestures with her finger for me to turn around and then back to the front. Two old ladies walk by. You can see my nipples through my bra. They look absolutely disgusted. I'm pretty sure it's illegal to strip-search me in the street but it doesn't seem to be the right moment to mention it.

– Put your top back on then, Jenni.

– Both of them?

– Yes.

– My sneakers?

– Hurry up, we'll finish this down at the station.

Clothes are so welcome when you've been out of them. The warmth of a T-shirt and hoody and then I am walking in front of her and him (there's only a few polis here) and we go down to the station like some strange little procession. I am on display so all the locals know the polis have got me, they are safe another day from the children's home kids.

– In you go.

The policeman opens the station door. Reception is bright. There are posters everywhere. Three for health and safety, one for a missing cat with little stubs of paper, a flyer for a local gardener. I expect to see my face up there. Do not let your children play with this child. She will get them high. This isn't paranoia. The police have phoned around various different kids' parents in the village and warned them not to let their sainted offspring hang out with me. It's a total fucking cheek as well because it's the local most esteemed vicar's son who is getting us all high, at no small profit.

– Where's she going today?

– I'll do it in cell 2.

A slight look between them. The guy on the front desk buzzes us through a big clunking door. It clangs behinds us. Walk carefully down a concrete hall that echoes even with rubber soles. The tread of both of us going past cell doors.

I am ushered into a concrete room. The toilet has no lid on it, barely even a rim. There is a bench also made of concrete and a tiny window with thick square glass panes.

– Okay, take your top off, jeans and bra this time as well.

– I don't have anything on me.

– Shut up! You don't get to say no to me in here, Jenni. You don't ask me questions, you speak when you are spoken to and you will do exactly what you are fucking told.

Pockmarks spike up all over my skin. The police officer walks around me in a circle as I unclip my bra. She reminds me of the girl in the caravan park who was way older and stuck her fat slobbering cow tongue into my mouth when I was about six.

– You won't make any friends around here. There is a local campaign to shut the children's home down, you do know that?

– I do.

– There's signs up – NO CARE HOME HERE!

– We see them.

– You lot lower the property prices the minute you turn up.

– Do I have to take my jeans off?

– Yes. The village has put together a petition and submitted it to the council to shut your kids' units down for good, you're not wanted here.

– We aren't wanted anywhere.

She stares at me.

– Socks, everything, all the way this time, just knickers only.

– Great.

– All the parents know who you are, so don't think you can go to any of their houses.

– Right.

– You'll be selling drugs, won't you? Or stealing.

– I'm not a thief.

The policewoman comes up really close into my face and stares at me for ages – then she slowly reaches forward and pulls my knickers out at the front.

– What's down here?

She peers down for a long minute.

I can see fine hairs on her lip and the grey of her eyes and a smell of coffee and mint on her breath – she lets the elastic snap back.

– Bend over.

– What?

Feel the heat of rage on cold skin.

– I'll find where you've stashed the drugs next time. We can pick you up off the street and strip-search you any time we want from now on, you do know that?

I dress in silence.

After they let me go I am so straight. Nothing is good. I want to disappear. There are no safe places. Anywhere. Not really. I go up to the vicar's son's house to worship my religion. Weed. It's a big fancy place cos pimping God does well and your kid selling gear is never going to send him to hell. My dealer opens the door. There are long thin rugs in the hall. Polished wood. Clean carpets. Old things! His room is at the front so we just turn right and go in. We never see the vicar. He is doing godly things. I've never once seen his mum either. I imagine they are nice people and their wasted son is just taking the absolute fucking piss. His room is full of music and weights and posters and sweetie wrappers.

– Where have you been, Jenni?

– Nowhere.

– Skin up then.

– Okay.

– You look pretty, you know that?

I didn't expect that.

He kisses me while I'm skinning up, then he takes the joint and gives me blowbacks, one after the other. This will be the fourth time I've done it. There was one dealer before this and it wasn't bad or good or anything really. I actually fancy this guy though. He is tall and skinny and listens to good music. Not sure I want to. Does anyone? It's quick. Sort of okay I suppose if you are into that sort of thing. I'm dazed. The door goes as he hauls up his boxers and jeans. It is a girl from up in the village. She comes in and sits down and looks tense. Holy fuck. She knows what we've been doing and I had no idea until this minute that she was his girlfriend. She has blonde hair and lots of spots but she is really cute. Much more so than him and then he's giving her a kiss and smiling at me to make sure I don't say anything and I have that feeling when you know someone has cheated you out of something you can't get back and you feel like an absolute fucking idiot. What's worse is she seems really nice!

– I don't eat food, she says.

– No?

– Well, only Curly Wurlys or toffee yogurt, nothing else, for two years now, I have entire drawers of Curly Wurlys – my parents gave up, didn't they?

He nods and smiles at her.

– Tell her about when you got busted, she says to him.

– It was bad.

– By the local polis?

– Aye, they bowled in, at the door, hammering away.

– What happened?

196

He exhales a joint and sticks it in his mouth back to front and gives her a long hot blowback and then another to me, it burns my throat and I feel the heaviness settling in me, arms move slower, colours brighter.

– My dad grabbed my weed, I mean fuckloads of it, had just had a delivery ay, and then he buried it in the back garden of the vicarage.

– Your dad, the vicar?

– I have never been so fucking proud of him!

The two of them are in hysterics.

It's raining when I walk home.

I go past the police station and over the bridge.

A kid came home to the unit the other day with no trainers cos the 'nice' village kids took them off him. They all want to fight us, fuck us, or fuck us over. Local kids' perks. The polis will always back them up and their families cos they are from here and they are good people and to them – we are not.

Walk through the woods in the dark on my own.

Back up to the unit where lights are on.

Into the pool room so I can get a game of pool before bed.

I put Pink Floyd on the record player.

Dark Side of the Moon is such a great album – indie music can't touch it. 'Comfortably Numb' lilts in and everything is good for now – overall. I pot the last ball. Walk back through the unit and go up to the middle landing.

There are bars on this window.

I put my hand up on the cold metal and think about how many kids have stood here before me looking out.

Head back out cos it's not late yet really and the girl with brown eyes meets me at the green gate with a bottle of vodka and another of Bacardi, we buzz some poppers and I drink my whole bottle straight and fall in a bush and when we get back

I have to sneak upstairs so the staff don't see me – I have to get my bath!

Look at my feet still down there at the end of my legs and they are bony!

I like my toes though – that's pretty lucky, to have nice feet.

Slip down into the water and down, down, down – time is out there somewhere.

Here under the water everything feels so nice.

The world is blissfully far – it's so warm and dark and within seconds I am … gone.

Bang.

Bang.

Bang.

BANG! BANG! BANG!

Someone kicks the door to the bathroom in.

I am dragged up out from under the water and smacked onto the floor soaking and ungainly as a newborn.

My mouth is opened.

Air.

Blown.

In.

I cough up water and splutter it everywhere as my throat burns and the room spins and spins.

67

I hide poetry like drugs. Scribble it on bits of paper. Stash it where the staff or other kids won't find it. I have whole books of it. Diaries too but I don't tell anyone. When I move it gets put at the bottom of bin bags, then under my mattress, or right under the dresser. Words are the only things that travel with me. Not even my name. I've been thinking about that lately. How they kept changing even that. How the me – I arrived as – was rebranded, altered, fucked up.

Then I'd have to move on as some new person.

Now I try to better myself every time I leave a place but it isn't working.

I got back from running away again just last night. It is every few weeks, or maybe every second month. Feel it building. Have to go. Walk streets all night on my own. Sleep in doorways, roundabouts, bushes, graveyards. Mostly I sleep rough in Edinburgh. I think it would be easier to scream and be heard in a city. No more viaducts for me. The unit is easy to light up into a wee riot too. Just like flicking the head of a match. Flash! A certain gaze and that's it – we are rioting. Smash the whole place up. It's never actually meant. We're not total pricks. There's things happening though. Here, in the unit, and in other places, and the kids tell me things that make me hurt for them, like whose mum is on the game and turns up high and things they've seen and one whose whole family have HIV including their little baby sister and brother, and it makes me want to cry but I stopped doing that. I know what someone's uncle has done, or a taxi driver, to a girl of thirteen, or how tiny kids were trained to go through pub windows and unlock the doors from the inside, or brothers who will never be convicted, or fathers, some who were made to watch their mothers have their face smashed in, run after them as they were dragged around, pulped and mulched, or whose stepdads made their own kids watch while they raped them. Those kids can't not see those things in their heads for the rest of their lives and once they've told me I can't either. That hurt will travel with me until I die. Every story is a pain. I never feel nothing. It's so hard. Over and over, I bear witness to things I haven't gone through but I never tell anyone about my own. I'm the one they need to be able to listen. I am who they come to with the things they don't want to tell anyone else.

I always hear them.

They ask me for advice on dealing with the police or social workers.

They call me a lifer. Cos I've always been in care. The adoptions were not timeout from that for me. I never belonged. To belong you have to be with people who see – you. Nothing worked in my life and it is so overwhelming that I now can't remember the last time I wasn't high. Maybe when I was twelve? I am in a field right now bent over looking for skinny little mushrooms with a dark nipple on top. The field is big and green. Two boys from the village are ahead of me. I like them actually, they are funny and they don't hit on me. Not all guys are sick. All the ones here have really stupid nicknames though. Their friends were up the woods earlier, they were sort of okay. They all go to the local school. We had to fight some of the girls though cos they were being bitches and taxing little kids from the unit cos they thought it was funny. I don't like fighting one bit. I hate violence. I hate a lot of the other teenage boys cos they're so arrogant and entitled and twisted and full of some sallow kind of hatred they have to leak out on anyone they see as weak. Some of their mates were lying watching us as we walked past them earlier in the woods and they started calling out …

– Why don't you fuck us? Later? Come over to his place?

– I'd rather fucking kill myself.

– That's no very nice!

– Get fucked.

– I'm trying!

– Shove yer needle dick up yer fucking arse!

They go out their way to impress girls with families but seem to think girls from units are so desperate we will fuck anything and nobody will come looking for them no matter what they do to us. That is the issue. These two guys are nice though. They're not like that. They get embarrassed when their mates talk like that to me. They stand in front of me carefully eating handfuls of long thin mushrooms. They hold a handful out to me. We drink Coke to drown out the muddy weird taste. Sit and smoke a joint and chat shit until the ground begins to gently sway. Down and then up. The trees sound louder rustling their leaves and just like that I realise water is rushing by, the river next to us has a large steel pipe going across it and I feel like I'm hearing all sounds for the first time, birds calling out, our feet walking on the grass.

– We'll cross there.

The boys go first and I follow, crawling on the pipe watching water whoosh below me – white and fast – and I think I can hear parrots or maybe it's Jodi – the sound of water is so loud that this feels like I've gone right through the wardrobe in Narnia to a place that has always been waiting for me.

– Why have you stopped, Jenni?

I'm giggling.

– Shit!

– She's just come right up, hasn't she?

– Get off the pipe!

I let one leg hang down and the water is running so fast.

– This way, please, Jenni, you have to come over the rest of the pipe, it's better on this side!

There is a huge stone wall behind the boys, it reminds me of the Pink Floyd film, shuffle forward on my knees, stand up on the other side. There are two boys glue-sniffing by the wall. One holds out a bag.

– I don't buzz glue, it's lame.

– It'll bring you up faster.

Inhale, two, three times, and the wall gets bigger, more elongated, my hands are so tiny and my feet – look at them all the way down there, they are silly! We are laughing. Our guts ache. Everything is beautiful. I have to go back to the unit for tea. I must not act like I'm tripping! Sneak in through a side door at the unit like a tiny psychedelic burglar. Upstairs and I go into the room of a girl with short hair and a turned-up nose and she gives me a wooden Buddha (to keep) and lets me laugh at her curtains for a full hour. I keep throwing my fingers out so they elongate across the room. Her room-mate is the one who wears death metal T-shirts and gets injections because her body odour is bad.

– Dinner!

It is a big distorted voice.

I have to follow the other kids downstairs.

We sit at tables of like six, or four, the prison chef is there and the food is good here but they watch everything I eat and write it down because they think I don't eat enough and also cos I won't eat meat any more. I try to lift my fork. Food swirls on the plate. A member of staff is watching me furiously so I go out the room – into the cold little downstairs toilet and my nose starts bleeding, fuck!

This is it.

What a bad trip feels like.

Oh God!

My veins are pulsing so hard in my neck and at my feet there are bright red drops of blood.

Someone comes in and tells me they are taking me to the hospital.

– For a nosebleed?

– No, to prove you are on drugs, Jenni. This time we've really just had enough!

Into the social work minibus then with a face full of bloody toilet tissue and they've brought the girl with the brown eyes because we hang out so much they think she must be high if I am and she is totally and utterly not!

– I'm so, sorry!

I whisper it but it is loud and then the gnarl of the engine and into town, into A&E and bright lights and into a cubicle and being registered, girls from a children's home, drug abuse, high risk, assessed, a light shone in my eye. He thrusts out a paper rectangle box thing at me.

– You need to do a urine sample in here.

– Get fucked, really?

– Now!

I can hear a nurse in the cubicle across from me telling the other girl that she is good but I am not good, I am the bad one.

I don't know how to act at all.

The loo is tiny.

Assess the situation.

First, a little wee, then I put my finger under the tap until the water is lukewarm (not hot) and I fill up about another two-thirds of the box with that. Go out and hand it back to the doctor. After that we all drive home in silence.

In bed I watch films on the inside of my eyelids. Tiny fluorescent witches fly by in formations of three. One sticks her fingers up at me and flies away on her broomstick.

School is long the next day.

I smoke a joint before it starts and take a Valium and then I have to go into gym. I normally never do gym. I find any excuse not to do it. I have done since I was a little kid because I went through puberty when I was years younger than anyone else and had a stripe of hair on my back and hated my body but lately I don't really want anyone to touch me. I don't like to take my clothes off. I try to leave the past behind but it is clenched in my fists. So, being in a swimsuit among normal kids when I feel so far removed from all of them is traumatic. Water glitters. I have to dive (it's not a dive – it's a dead weight falling) head first to get away from the light and the noise and the cluster of szhoozh and energy and fakery and the way I feel weird whenever I spend too long around kids who like to talk about me like I just broke out of prison and I'm about to go back down any day now (this month is my third trip to the children's court) and I am down there under the muffled gurgle, pulling my hands through water and kicking my legs out like a fucked-up frog and trying to get this brick from the bottom of the pool but I am so high I am just swimming squint across the middle of the pool and wishing a tiny sinkhole would open up and swallow me. The gym teacher blows a whistle. I get out like a drowned reprobate. In the showers one of the girls who used to hate me but sort of loves me now but who is also obsessed with how many people I can fight and what it is like when I go missing and how much drugs I take and how many people talk about me – she says something about how I probably don't even have a decent right hook anyway and she goes to sort of hit her hand towards my face or something so I smack her and her nose spreads across her face and half a dozen naked girls start screaming as blood billows out in long red curls across the wet shower floor.

68

I'm the only kid in the unit who doesn't know anyone they are related to, or who has been in care as long as I have. I've been steeling myself to deal with Christmas on my own in here. I'm in the smoking room. None of my friends at school, or anyone, notices that I am just in a kids' unit at Christmas, not really. They don't ask me to go to their homes. None of them do. I don't bring it up that I'll be in a unit on my own because it's embarrassing. I hate it when anyone feels sorry for me. I get £36 Christmas allowance to go and buy myself a gift but I've not gone to get anything yet. I'm going to go up town later with the girl with brown eyes who is all heart and freckles and goodness. She wants to be a nurse when she leaves care, then have kids and get married. I hope she gets to do all of it.

She comes in and I move over so we can sit together and give her a cigarette.

– I'm not going home on Christmas Day, she says.

– What?

– I won't leave you in here on your own, Jenni, I'm going to spend it with you, ay. We'll have a totally brilliant day!

It's the kindest thing anyone has ever done for me.

If I could still cry I would.

Outside the police are pulling into the car park; they get out and put their hats on.

– Think that's yer groupies, she says.

The unit is lit up with different coloured lights in all the kids' bedrooms. I've been stealing coloured light bulbs from the big outdoor church Christmas tree. I climb up and dangle there and then unscrew another hot red or green or yellow bulb and later that day the vicar always replaces them. Sort of like a twelve days of Christmas game. It's the nice policeman that comes into the smoking room to see me. I double-drag and fidget with my sleeve.

– How many times have you been charged now, Jenni?

– Don't know.

– It's a lot.

– God loves a trier!

– Doesn't he just? Talking about God, the unit is all lit up in different colours!

– Bless the little children for they have nothing.

– Quite.

Try not to smile.

– Anyway, never mind that, Jenni, I need to speak to you about the police lights taken from our fleet of cars outside the station?

– I have no idea what you're talking about.

– Yes, you do, we've already interviewed you five times, there is the ongoing issue with someone removing the lights from police cars outside our station, they've been repeatedly stripped for months, all the stickers, police lights off the top, hub cabs, there are five or six, is it, missing lights? We have finally got a witness who said they saw you do it.

– Do what?

– Crouch on the top of a police car right outside the station with a screwdriver undoing a police light!

– This isn't a festive visit then?

– No, Jenni.

– Santa has me on his naughty list? I guess I won't be getting a shiny new bike with ribbons on the handlebars for Christmas?

– Not this year.

– The police are still trying to get me put in a secure unit, aren't they?

A shrug.

– That's not up to us really, Jenni. Everyone wants you to just be where you are safe and the thing about all of this is, it is a really serious crime to vandalise and steal police property, so, if you could get the lights back for us, for example, that would help you out a bit when we have to charge you for it.

Look at him, he is actually the only police person who has ever been kind to me.

– Can you give me twenty minutes?

– We can give you ten. Will you come to the station right afterwards?

– Okay.

I like this policeman, he's the only one I've ever liked. He's always splitting his trousers open and his girlfriend who works in the kids' home lets him in and sews them up. She can't stand me but he makes me want to maybe, I don't know, take it easier. I better be able to get those police lights back – I run all the way.

Knock.

The vicar's son answers with his girlfriend (he has been keeping them for me because he always wanted genuine police memorabilia but was too scared to nick any); they are helplessly giggling.

– I don't see what's fucking funny!

– Wait …

She is poorless with laughter, tears in her eyes, clutching at her stomach.

– You have to take them to the police station?

– Aye, like now!

I hold my hand out.

– We, well, we did a craft project!!

They go inside and get them. Come back to the door. Pass the lights over to me. I don't say a fucking word. Run down to the station with them in my arms. Get into the reception where the police are looking pretty fucking smug, drinking victory tea, waiting on me coming in to get charged (this charge might get me in secure which is what most of them have been wanting for ages), and I line all the police lights up on the counter one by one in a row – each one is spray-painted neon pink and covered in glitter.

The entire station stops.

We all share a respectful moment's silence.

Holy, holy!

Hallelujah!

Hark, the herald angels sing!

This moment is worth it even if they do lock me up.

The look on their faces!

Especially the bitch that strip-searches me.

Feels like one of the great triumphs of my life, like learning to drive or something.

Later I find out that the girl with brown eyes went in and said it was mostly her that did it so I won't get locked up in a secure unit; yet again, I have escaped and nobody knows how I keep managing to stay out and I think she is so decent and I wasn't stripping the cars for fun (solely), I was stripping them because they wouldn't stop stripping me. She takes the charge. They can't prove it wasn't her. It's a checkmate. We do that in the units sometimes. Take charges for each other, without hesitation. They know we do it but they can't do anything, and if it means I'm in a bedroom without furniture nailed to the floor and deadlocks on the door for a little while longer, then we have beaten them – for one more day.

69

Snow falls outside the unit. It is my favourite weather alongside autumn, when everything turns crisp, and there is always woodsmoke on the air. I love watching lights sparkle at night in the dark. It is magical. Snow quietens everything. It lays fat and white on the boughs of all the trees. I am looking out of my bedroom window. The lamp posts are not pretty here but I still think of Mr Tumnus with his parcels and umbrella walking through the snow whenever it's dark like this and snow is falling. Snow falls heavier and thicker and I smile imagining faun hooves leaving little horseshoe-shaped prints going down into the woods. I am still writing in secret every day. The lump on my finger from writing is big now. It will always be there I think. Words are the only thing that have always travelled with me, that I can turn to no matter what and when I feel like I am fragmenting – I write to find a part of me, and somehow it helps me come back to myself.

Curl up on my bed happy as a cat.

There isn't anything I like more than snowfall at Christmas. It's like the only present I need.

We are going to try and do something nice for the staff tomorrow as well.

In the morning we wake really late and it's quiet because everyone else is away.

Perfect.

Have breakfast downstairs and over the morning a few other members of staff pop in, who aren't even working today, they come in just to bring us little presents they've bought themselves. A silver chain, a pad, a book. They are being so nice to us. I feel bad for them sometimes cos they don't get to do the things they want half the time. To even do this they have to break the rules because their jobs are so hindered by policy. I really like them for doing it.

Little acts of resistance and kindness help save future lives.

We stay in pyjamas and slippers all day. We play stupid games. We play pool. We are so good at pool now we could be taken to any bar and filed in with our hoodies up and pretend we are old enough to be out gambling in the big halls and hustle for a ton of fucking cash. Last week the head of the social work department came out to the unit and had a meal with us. He grew up in care too. I quite liked him or at least I thought it was cool he'd come out and actually have tea with us but he's leaving soon. The new guy taking over the social work department is not good. That's what I've heard. None of that matters right now because we are at a Chinese takeaway (a rare treat) to get our dinner and we walk out with the plastic bags rustling and hot spicy food smelling so good on the way home and a feast for us and the two members of staff who have stayed on for the whole day and there is laughter, and really, when I think about it, they are all here for me today – the girl with the brown eyes could have gone home to her mum and the staff likely all have other places they could be too, I am the one who has nobody.

I am so fucking grateful.

In the afternoon we phone the radio station that we've been listening to Christmas songs on all day long. Me and the girl with brown eyes tell the radio station that we want to say a heartfelt thank you to the staff for making it a beautiful day for us. It's a surprise when our message is read out live on air and the staff roll their eyes but they are teary and we can tell it means a lot to them. It's good to thank someone when they do you a kindness. I grew up on fairy tales. I know what manners mean. You don't let someone do good for you and not let them know.

70

Five police cars flew out to our unit from three different departments. We barricaded ourselves in my bedroom with my wardrobe. It all started because I accidentally smashed my bedroom window – I was getting changed and one of the boys was on the roof next to my window, watching me get dressed. I just wanted to give him a fright! I only meant to hit the window but the whole thing smashed and then someone screamed downstairs and then the whole place went up in total chaos. Other things have been happening. I slept with a man. He had a seventies car. It went fast. He had a friend. The girl with the brown eyes wanted to be with the friend forever and she said it was love and she meant it. They worked on nearby land. The one I slept with had a photograph of his sister on his dresser. I had to move it because she was the same age as me which made shagging him feel creepy. The police found us there. They dragged us out. The man who I slept with went back to England. He got done for murder. He's in prison now. I have been sleeping on the streets all over town for the last few months. On my own, hooded top pulled up. It feels more honest for me to be on the streets than anywhere else lately. Even in the unit there is a cold in my bones that I can't get out and there's staff that hate me even if it's just some of them and I can't walk down the high street without a police car trailing behind me if they see me. A lot of people want me in a secure unit now but there is never a space, it's like some fucking angel is looking out for me cos they know the day I get locked up I will have to find another way to leave. I left the unit three nights ago and two of the boys followed me. I don't like running away with anyone else – I only like going on my own. I told them sleeping rough is shit fun! They followed me. They were adamant. I didn't want them to come. I can walk all night when I am sleeping rough on my own and it's the only time I don't feel like I have to answer to anyone, or like I'm a burden, or a bit of fucking charity to pity. In my life there are always eyes on me and most of them not for good reasons. It gets really tiring being me. I just want an armchair I can read in and to hug my teddy and take naps for about ten years. My neck hurts all the time. There are marks on my fists from where those big needles went in when I took the overdose. I think of those guys at the river and what happened whenever I wash my own clothes. There are little white scars on the inside of my arms and inner thighs where I have tried to let the pain out. I keep trying to forget but my body won't stop telling me what happened to it. Wherever I go when I run away I have learned to always walk by back roads and rivers and woods and find my own places to stay and I never let any guys talk to me for one minute ever. It was a pain having the boys come along with me. I had to worry about them. We were found trying to hot-wire a car (it's the red wire or is it the blue or the brown and the green?), I'm fucking rubbish at hot-wiring, but we were getting there and then security outside a nightclub chased us and then the police ran down after us on the railway and caught us and dragged us into a city station and at first we wouldn't give them our names.

Both of the boys got battered in another room – until a call came through.

– There are three children missing from a Midlothian children's home, fitting your description …

When we got back to the unit the boys were jumping around telling the staff they wanted the police charged and I was the only witness so now I am sitting in the staff flat across from our unit with a Chief of Police or a Superintendent or a Big Bad Bastard Who's the Boss, he sits really relaxed with his legs spread wide and a calm look on his face.

– And when you got back to the unit the boys said they were going to have the policemen who, allegedly, assaulted them arrested for it? What do you think about that, Jenni?

– The youngest boy is twelve years old, there were bruises on both of them, if they want me to testify I will.

He takes his hat off.

It's placed on the sofa.

I try not to think about what I've heard two members of staff have done with kids here.

They don't work here any more.

Nobody talks about it.

He pulls himself up straighter to look down on me.

– Those men have children, wives and families to support. If you testify against them we will have you locked up in a secure unit before the month is out and you have no family so there won't be any weekend visits, you won't get out on your birthday, or Christmas, you will be in a secure unit 24/7 for years.

– I see.

– Make your choice in the next hour and let the staff know. I will send a police car to pick you up right away, depending on what you decide.

He trudges out, smiles to the staff, they make polite chit-chat, he leaves, probably going to play golf or something. The boys want to know what happened.

– They say that they will get me locked up in a secure unit if I testify, but I will, if you want me to.

– No.

– No!

– We don't want to press charges then, the boys say.

I am relieved and embarrassed and furious.

My anger is root-deep.

Feel it in the snap of my tone, the lack-of-any-fucks-given. I feel it when I pull my knickers back up. I feel it when I see Monroe one day and realise she is losing herself to the mush of chemicals and arseholes. I see it when my headmaster pulls me into his office and holds out his hand (with a tissue on it) for my nose studs for the fourth time this year. I feel it when the piercing gun puts a hole in my skin. When I walk out into oncoming traffic one morning because a squirrel is getting run over again and again. Hold my hand up. Cars beep at me! Morning commuters are so angry! I ignore them and take off my school cardigan and scoop up a half-dead squirrel and walk it up to the woods (cars still beeping behind me) and its brains fall out when I unwrap it and then I bury it. I feel it in the street lights spilling orange on rain, the crack of bone, a fight between the brown-eyed girl and pat-a-pat-pat of feet, of desperate feet, pushing along the ground, the slay of spit and sirens, the deep sob, I feel it in the bloodlust of teenagers all shout-shout-shout-shout when they watch a fight go down and I feel it in the way kids watch me walk down a school corridor. How they talk about me when I'm not there. I feel it in the dealers' houses I go into, to pick up, to sell gear or tabs or whatever at the sheds near our school, in the eyes of boys and older guys, in the creak of a gate. I feel it when I'm too high. I feel it in my hunger and my jut-hips. In the way I used to curl my nails into my fist to leave half-moons, then tried out razors.

I feel it when I smash or set fire to anything. I feel it in every report that was ever written about me since I was born, it's all been documented – everything, that is, except for the hideous, vile things that have happened over and fucking over again, to me.

71

The only member of staff that really doesn't like me has short curly brown hair and a pretty face. Mostly everyone likes me. Lots of the staff do. They despair and stuff but I am still smart and I'm funny and weirdly, considering all the other things I do, I don't actually directly give them any shit. If a kid is threatening one of them I'll snap at them to stop it. This place is just a job for some aye and most of them are doing the best they can. I mean there were two abusers worked here but there isn't any of them abusing kids in here just now. Not that I know of anyway and I am pretty sure I would be the first one to hear. The staff office always smells of Pledge furniture polish and cheap furniture.

– Just like I say, it's a unit quite far from here, it will give her some independence and she will buy her own food and get ready to leave care and we have found you a foster family.

– What?

– You can't stay here any more.

– Why?

– You can't stay in a unit forever, Jenni!

– Why not?

– Don't you want to try and live with a family again?

– No.

– Jenni, you have become so tough about everything. There is something wrong ... with you. You don't cry, you don't show any emotion, you don't eat unless it's a vegetable and even then not often, the police charge you at least once a week and you walk out of the office afterwards like they just read you a goodnight story, you have become too … hard. It won't be much longer until you won't be able to make it back even if you want to.

Tick.

Tick.

Tick.

The clock goes this way and that way. There are clocks on the grass outside the kids' unit. I see them when I am tripping.

Tick.

Tick.

Tick.

So, the brown-eyed girl who was the one person in here I cared about is gone.

Now, they are getting rid of me.

Worse.

Everything she says is right.

I prided myself on becoming someone who doesn't cry any more.

Like when my voice went … another part of me has been drifting further away.

Needed to put it safe.

Somewhere far away from me …

– You have been charged more than any other child we have ever cared for here, you can start a riot just by blinking, you are the brain behind everything in here!

– That's insulting!

– To who?

– Everyone fucking else who lives here!

– It's true. What I am trying to say, Jenni, is that you are a highly unusual case.

– So, I'm moving when?

– In a few days …

– Are you shitting me?

She picks up her keys to head outside.

– I shit you not!

I go to the smoking room and light up.

One of the little kids comes in and he grins at me.

– How come you always look like that, Jenni?

– Like what?

– Classy, like you wear weird-as-fuck stuff honestly like you do but you always look super fucking – CLASSY!

– Thank you.

– You do. You always look amazing – does someone teach you that? How to do it?

– No.

– I bet you even smell like strawberries.

He says it real quiet and goes upstairs to his bed. I sit on my own with my lighter just spinning it round and round and watching the flash of it in the dark and one of the new boys comes in, he is leaving soon too.

– You don't want to sit there with a lighter looking like that!

– Why?

– Last time I had the kind of vibe you have right now … I burnt the disabled kids' school down. Don't look at me like that, Jenni – what are ye, the PC police? Nobody was fucking in it at the time!

He goes off to the office just a young, elegant pyromaniac. In a unit you think you're close to everyone but really you are not, it is transient. You'd die for each other one day and never speak to each other again the next. I go upstairs and begin to pack my stuff into the same old bin bags. Smile to myself remembering playing chicken in cars on the farm roads. I climbed out the window when they were driving and held on to the windscreen as the car went faster and faster. Or when the cars drove towards each other at full speed and it was really fucking uncertain if we would die or not and how I went joyriding on acid that one time and how I am a different me every time I leave a place – from the one I was when I arrived.

Truth is I don't have a fucking clue, really, as to who I am.

I'm a moving thing.

A written-about selection of names, and numbers, sitting in a locked filing cabinet, in the cold.

72

I find out the girl with the brown eyes from the last unit is at a homeless accommodation place near here. Not really totally homeless but a sort of in-between place, learning how to cook pasta and budget before you move out of care kind of vibe. I walk up there from the new foster parents'. Through two other council estates than the one I'm living on, then down a hill to where lots of massive high-rises dot their way down the slopes. I go up a wee path and chap on the door of a small single-level grey building.

– Jenni, it's so fucking good to see you!

– You too!

I'm giddy-happy as I follow her and she takes me past her room (tiny with wee kitchen bit in it) then through to the living room where a stoned girl is eating crisps and the utter joy of playing Mario and Sonic – jaggy spears fly out of Sonic so he loses his coins. We sit. Just three girls, rolling joints and smoking steadily and playing computer games and having a laugh. It's everything. Then she wants to go down to the high-rise flats to pick up. The high-rises are like five big fingers sticking up at the sky. They have windows all the same size with curtains or nothing on or lights or a flower. I wait in the graffiti bit outside a lift and a guy with a bald head comes up to me.

– I've heard about you, he says.

– Oh, aye?

– Aye.

– What did you hear?

– I heard you hate the police more than anyone. If you want I'll let you pick up some gear for me, drop it off? Give you a bit of weed for it?

– Aye, fine.

– I need you to pick up some fake cash when you are in there as well then, the guy prints them in his flat and it costs £4 for a twenty so I make £16 per note, you look like a nice lassie, maybe take a few earrings out and go up town, spend each twenty getting something cheap in a shop – get real money in return?

– Maybe.

– Come up, I'll take you in to meet him.

We go up in the lift. It stinks of piss. On the first floor we can hear tellies and some kid screaming at his sibling and the gentle thud of the lift as it closes behind us. He knocks three times, stands back. We go into a flat with a hallway rammed with boxes of stereos and videos and lots of cat food for some reason and in the living room there is a guy sitting in front of a money press – crisp green notes fall into a neat pile.

– Who is she?

– She's going to do a few things fir me, you do this …

He crunches up a note, rubs it together, flattens it out, then hands it to me.

– Okay.

– Feels more real if you scrunch them, they look amazing but it's the feel of them, just a tiny bit thicker than normal money.

The guy printing the money eyes me up and grins and behind him *Countdown* is placing down letters. I try to work out if it could spell – fucked.

– Take a couple of notes, see how you go, come up and see me once you've made money on them, and if you do okay, I might gie ye some more?

– Okay.

He hands me a couple of fake notes.

Downstairs I find the girl with the brown eyes smoking with some guy; there's a group of about forty kids all hanging around down at the bottom of the flats now, a skinhead is shouting at everyone.

– Stay the fuck back!

– Dinnae dae this tae me!

A guy is trying to back away and the energy is dark as hell cos you can see the power in the guy that is going to do him in and he's an absolute fucking psycho.

– Any cunt steps in and ye'll fucking get it …

They crack the guy's head open and then lay into him with their feet.

I head away two more high-rises down and ride up in the lift on my own because the guy said to go to another flat to get the gear. Lights flicker. Some old lady gets in, she is skinny and hard as fuck – it's an aura that steps into each space before them when someone is genuinely like that – it announces their arrival – so you know to adjust your demeanour to – no fucking threat to anyone yet still not a soft cunt.

– They keep riding on the top of the lifts! she says.

A wee bony old-lady finger points at the hatch above us.

– Really?

– Aye, they climb up into the lift shafts then jump from one lift onto the other one flying up on the opposite side! So, there's a drop up tae ten floors and a gap like fucking yon size …

The woman holds her hands about four feet apart.

224

– That's bad!

– Aye, one guy got fucking caught, by his jeans, on a fucking hook, arsehole, he was wearing Levi's, reckon they jeans fucking saved him, he should have got Levi's tae sponsor him, life-saving jeans and that, aye?

The lift pings.

I glide up one more floor. All the people I come from started out in places like these. So did I for that matter. We were in the highest high-rises in the country I think. The ones that get lit up so planes don't take the top-floor flat out when they are coming in for a landing. A guy is waiting for me outside another flat. I stay silent as he knocks on the door and it clunks open. It has automatic bolts all the way around the door. It's a safe house! Wee thrill. I've never been in one before. The police can't break the doors down in these ones. They tend to be addresses not known to anyone. Down a bare hallway. This flat that has not one single dot of furniture in any of the rooms. No carpets. Totally clean. It's been hoovered. We go into the living room. Around all four walls are stacks of guns. Big long guns. All the way up the walls to about my chest height maybe. In the kitchen another guy cuts out some red bar, some gold bar and a sheet of LSD. I take what I'm being told to sell, say ta and go back out like I didn't see a thing. Skin up in the lift on the way down, super quick, light up as I walk out and my friend is there, finished whatever she was doing.

– When was the last time you werenae high every day, Jenni?

Look up at the moon, wee fingernail in the sky, we used to be friends her and me and the stars don't shine here so much because there is too much light from the flats and the roads and the city nearby. I miss that about the last unit – trees and stars and darkness and space!

– Dunno, when I was eleven I suppose if I really think about it, or twelve actually more like? Couldn't always score every single day then.

– Fuck's sake, Jenni.

– I never see you any more, what the fuck have you been up to?

– Been hanging out with some woman up town. Are you still going to school?

Her eyes go dark when she mentions the woman and I get a cold feeling but I know better than to ask more.

– Not often, they put me on work experience though, in the hairdresser's – you know how they say what job you are capable of doing – they've said I'll be lucky if I even manage that and they are fucking right, it is sore being on your feet all day and listening to all those clients talking utter pish. My boss asked me when me and him were going to fuck-fuck!

– Gross. You are clever as fuck though! How come they've made you do a hairdresser's?

– Don't think the solicitors want me there!

We both begin laughing, all the way up the road, sniggering away to ourselves, this weed is really good. She is safe and happy. That was all I wanted to know after she left that last unit. On my walk home I route out the new streets in my head so I don't have to think about it next time. It's what I do when I move. Work out where I am. How to get back. Where the bus stops are. If there are any shortcuts and then try not to panic because sometimes I worry I'm going to move somewhere and get high and then just not know how to get back to whatever house I'm living in because I can't even remember the way.

Back at my new foster parents we sit together and smoke and watch telly.

It's nice actually.

The mum has a good face but wouldn't take any shit and they've two Dobermanns and there are a lot of people in the house but they are good people and I don't want to fuck them around. Go upstairs and hide my shit. Try to stay awake. I don't like falling asleep. I have nightmares. The same shadow man is chasing me. Rapists with shows transmitting everything they ever did to a girl, and the person in their guest chair, who they did it to – is me. There's no social workers in my dreams. They barely turn up in my life. Haven't seen mine in about six months. Nobody. Not a peep. I rang the department and it turns out she left ages ago and nobody noticed I hadn't been allocated a new one. The woman on the phone said, oh, oh, okay, we will get back to you. It does not matter. The last time I had a social worker who actually connected with me I was three and a half, since then it's sort of organisational admin of getting me from one place to another, and I couldn't say I'd ever had a real conversation with any of them. Maybe it's just me. I hung out in my school library yesterday. Sneaked in. Made sure nobody noticed. I didn't think the librarian would tell anyone. Found some books I hadn't read. *A Clockwork Orange*, and *The Color Purple* by Alice Walker. I skived off and fell totally in love with the voice of Celie – could see her sitting in houses totally unseen, just this young black girl in the South when they were still doing lynching, and it got to me. It really, really got to me. I am a bit embarrassed because I should be doing well at school. I have fallen so far from all of that and I don't know how I will ever make it happen now but maybe someday I can live somewhere with a wee quiet space for me to study again.

73

I haven't seen the girl with brown eyes for months. She just disappeared. I am bored and at a loose end when the guy I've been selling stuff for asks me to go up there and get high with him. A new social worker came to see me this morning and said that my last adoptive family want their name back and to unadopt me.

– What will my name be then?

– What do you mean?

– What will you call me?

– Eh. She sat with her pen in mid-air clearly having not considered that.

– There isn't another name for me – should I just pick one?

– Let me get back to you on that.

– Okay.

Names. Numbers. Workers. Files. Foster families. Meetings. Liaisons. The kids' court. Doctors. School. Teachers. Headmaster. Police. Kids' homes. Buses. New roads, new places to remember. New shops. New streets. New doors. New rooms. When will I leave? Bin bags always in the drawers. Eyes watching. Nobody noticing anything. Sitting in the woods on my own when I should be in class trying to see if I can catch a glimpse of the old forest people in the trees. The guy's flat is okay. I trust him now, sort of. Go up there and get high. He listens to me talk a lot. Seems to like it. Tries to find out as much about me as he can when I get the feeling with so many of the people I live with or who worked with me the goal was to absolutely avoid that in case I said something they didn't want to have to do something about.

I don't know.

Maybe I'm wrong.

I have a new social worker again now anyway.

The guy lives up in the top high-rises where the ice-cream man does deals from the van and there's this nice woman but she gets her baby stoned – like just a little bit. She blows weed smoke over the kid's head so it sleeps, even a dog got wasted here cos it ate a quarter by mistake and when it puked it up it was just a white fibre husk. Sometimes it feels like everyone is off their tits. Even the old people are pissed up or on sleeping tablets. I guess all the nice people in the high-rises who live straight decent lives are hiding from folk like us. He answers the door in grey tracksuit bottoms and bare feet.

– Don't you look fucking stunning!

– Whatever.

I'm wearing jeans, T-shirt, little black lace choker around my neck. I follow him down the hall and he beckons me into the kitchen where he's got a whole set-up – bong – sink – some wraps – he thrusts silver foil under my nose and lights a flare of red so it's reflected in both our eyes.

– Inhale!

I take the little pipe and a chemical, bitter and acrid, burns my throat.

Don't even know what I've just smoked.

– Thanks.

I can't break that habit of being polite, people like it or they don't – I was thinking about it on the way here – I shouldn't totally give up on having pals my own age who don't do all this stuff. Maybe if I could join a writing group? Just not tell anybody. Or a drama group. Maybe I could make friends with people my own age who I could talk to about books and music and clothes and art. Maybe someone nice might want to date me, like not a drug dealer, or a murderer, maybe someone who was just like funny and sweet and we could go to the cinema and hold hands and I could just be – me.

What normal guy would want me though? After all of it. And the thing is whenever I'm not stoned, I hurt – so badly – so, I'll get stoned just this once more and then I am going to straighten up. I don't want to live this life any more. I want my mind properly back. I don't know what he's got me smoking but I am floating already.

– Now, we have all of this for madam ... look, I prepared it all earlier.

This is the dealer version of someone making a picnic.

He's set the sink up for the bong, there is a half-ounce on the side of that with red seal, gold seal, grass, there are tablets enough for Alice in Wonderland.

– Are you still taking the acid, Jenni?

– Aye.

I drop the acid tab that he gives me on my tongue and then I turn to accept the plastic bottle he has swirled up – totally full of smoke, he holds it forward looking at me sideways.

– You need to do the whole lot.

– Not a problem.

Rising to the challenge is what I do. I am nothing if not resilient. I learned to always try as hard as I could at everything. I take the entire bong. Pause twice to exhale. Then he is straight swirling up another one, and another, then another, until the world is dark outside, and stars rise somewhere out there across deserts and seas and mountains and here all the high-rises are lit up. I go through into the living room. There is nothing except for a sofa, a stereo and a table for skinning up on.

– What did you do before?

It's like the sound around us has gone like pinball machines at the fairground. All bright and chattery and echoey and I try to look really sober and really straight like I always do when I realise I am way too high.

– Before what, Jenni?

– I dunno.

There is a sound like a dull metal ball falling down a derelict well.

My legs are numb.

So is my back – it feels in fact like half my body is gone.

Everything begins – to fade.

Last week somebody told me that he had a whorehouse before he did this. Then he was in prison. He says I always give him good advice on what to do! I am trying to form words but colours rush in towards me.

I don't know what he gave me!

Just as I register what is happening his mouth turns up in a little smile.

Heartbeat fast.

Can't see!

I slide down the wall.

Paralysed.

Can't move at all.

Colours are so bright and his face is really grinning at me now through them for a minute too – then it disappears as well.

I am travelling at high speeds now but my body is unable to move.

He props me up against the wall.

Little slouch doll.

Door goes.

Footsteps walk down the hallway, lots of them, guys, my stomach drops as I try to count the footsteps, count them, count things, count everything, they walk into the bare room and stand in a line in front of me. I'm sort of leaned back against the wall and I can't see through the colours but I have crystalline audio vision and I am counting four men (or five) and then also there is him and my heart is going so fast and I need to somehow show them that I am in here but I can't move my body and I can't see.

Fuck! Fuck! Fuck. Bad. Bad. Bad. Bad. Bad. Bad. Bad. Bad. BAD. BAD. BAD. BAD!

I must try to breathe.

– Fuck's sake, check the state of her, tidy wee ride but!

– What's she hud?

– Everything.

Someone clicks their fingers near my head.

Try to twist my head towards the sound but I can't see a fucking thing.

Can't speak either – I am trying to fight my way back through the colours but they are everywhere and I am falling through the floor – they are saying words that warble then I hear one of them pulling down their zip.

– Do whatever you want, the whole works.

– Fucking A!

Heart pounding I drag myself a centimetre up the wall in a total fear-filled freakout – hands floundering around on the dirty floor. I can't believe this is happening. You walk into a room and someone starts a thing. At a kitchen bunker. In a house. Nobody else home. It starts the thing and you can't stop it. Someone pounding down a hallway towards me. Leaving my body. Tiny and hungry with sores all over me. I am getting flashes of my past and trying to ignore them and get back to myself as one of the men takes a step forward.

– What age is she?

– She is fucking old enough, fucking beautiful wee cunt as well, check the tits on it!

It's the bald guy that I've been friends with over all these months that is doing the talking.

– Move her so she's lying down, fuck's sake, aye!

– Wait!

It's the guy who asked what age I was.

A tiny blade of light in my heart …

Soon it will be time to go back to my real home.

I won't survive this. If they take turns, I know with complete fucking clarity I won't make it back. I can't go through anything like this again, I can't, and I know it and it will be time to go home. That wasn't ever on this planet. I call out to my angels and the ones who met me on the other side last time and I ask them to be here for me now, I won't get through this alone. I don't want to be here. I don't fucking want to be in a world where this stuff keeps happening to people any more. I don't know what is wrong with humans. It just makes me want to die.

– Fucking wait fir what?

– I didnae think you meant like this.

– Like fucking what?

Two of the men begin to square up to each other over my body in the living room and the other guys are silent.

– She looks about fucking ten years old, she's totally fucking gone … and I know her foster brother, he'd fucking kill the lot ay youz for this.

– Would he fuck!

– I'm no doing it … no like this.

One set of feet walk out of the flat and down the hall.

All of the high-rises glow so radioactive it can be seen right across space and time and the tiny circle of colour I was trying to still see through grows smaller and smaller until the whole world turns black.

74

So many days have passed. The colours kept me a long time.
First my arms return. Keep staring through the reds and blues
and purples and pinks and greens until his face appears.

Eyes first.

Then a spiteful mouth in a stocky meathead.

I am tiny, raw-boned, hollow-bodied.

Even although he dresses younger, he is a man. Not a boy,
not a teenager, he's not even in his twenties. I hadn't really
noticed it before now. I see a thick flabby neck. He smokes a
joint and stares. Over and over and over he says things. Points
with his spliff, jabs it towards me to punctuate his words.

– Yer just a wee dirty, ay? A wee fucking dirty from a home.

Can't quite speak yet. My eyes are cavernous. Two huge
holes in my face. I look down at my hands. They are bird hands
made of bone. Craggy and ancient! I can't fight him. So she is
coming. I feel her descend from all the way out there – make
her way through decades and days and sorrows and sins and
thousands of Sundays – she has come to take over my body
and do battle with this man for me. I feel her literally settle
into my fourteen-year-old body. As we fuse together my limbs
are those of a seventy-three-year-old woman.

She's sending me away.

Off out somewhere else where I'll be safe.

It's her game now.

My future self is not scared of him but she knows I am not
getting through this.

A slow smile on my face.

Something flickers across his eyes.

Like he can see her.

I reach my hands up towards the vast caves of my eyes and tiny birds fly out the sockets. Cavernous holes in my face. Tiny black birds fly out in every direction. We are every age we will ever be. Time is not static. It goes forward. It goes back. She is not leaving my mind to be raped by him any more.

It's what he is doing.

Doesn't even try to hide it.

– I will fuck your head and your body and then you will be owned. Won't you? Crazy fucking bitch. You know they are going to come and take you away in a wee white van? Lock you up. Unless I stop them. Don't look at me like that, hen, nae cunt is coming to save you. That white van is driving here right now. Aye, it is! You are going onto the nut ward for fucking life unless you do what I say.

Ash falls off the end of his joint.

The room is leaving again.

His legs, his fists, his eyes, the sofa, the walls – I go out into the way beyond.

It's where she keeps me safe.

My future self is not scared of anything.

I travel through colours for days, hours, flashes of the room here and there, the clock spinning, both hands, round and round and round and round faster and faster, sun comes up, moon goes down, there are people in the outside world but I can't go there, not again, my body is growing younger – she tugs me back down, she's leaving. She can't stay here for too long or she might not get back again either.

I feel empty when she is gone.

So – lonely.

Dirty.

Unclean!

My skin is all cold and pale and blotched and grimy.

Coming back into myself I have a strong urge to flutter my hands across my body to check for bruises but I do not dare move a muscle in front of him.

– So, you – owe me, he says.

– O – kay. Okay!

My voice is this tiny husk. I can't remember the last time I spoke. What I am getting from this minute is that I am going to make it back out of that door which before now I wasn't sure would ever happen unless I was dead. I suppose dead child prostitutes don't make so much money and it turns out that is what this whole thing has been for, he wants me on the game so he designed the entire thing to break me.

Broken people do what they are told.

– You'll come here, certain hours, do what I say? I'll get a red light. I'll split you like 70/30 so you'll get some money, aye. Customers will come downstairs, you'll do it in the back bedroom. Red light. Whatever they want. They leave. You get a bath. Go back to your foster parents. What do you say?

– I have to go home for a wee while, my foster parents will have reported me missing, the polis will be looking for me, what day is it?

Whispering still, my voice cracked, panicking still that I won't ever make it out of this flat alive.

– What are you going to tell them about where you've been?

– I was at a party.

Nods. If I want to leave alive he will take what he thinks he is owed, or at least some of it before I go, what is he owed? His money's worth? For what? I don't know who I am any more. I've been a lot of places and there were many people. I want to walk out of there alive. Play nice. Be nice. Smile nice. Act nice. Be sweet. Don't look him in the eye directly. I don't know what fucking happened to me. I was going to be a clean bright thing in a brilliant world, a scientist maybe.

At some point later on that day the front door all the way down at the end of that hallway gets opened …

Fly out.

Into the lift hauling on clothes.

Through early-morning streets and judging by papers at the newsagent's it has been days since I left my foster parents and when I get back she is pissed off and the police arrive and I sit in the kitchen staring.

– Where have you been then, Jenni, ay?

I couldn't even answer that if I tried.

Don't talk to the police.

Never did.

Just sit there chain-smoking cigarettes while they lecture me and I hear the sound of someone's zip and around the fringe of the kitchen there is a flood of colours, threatening to dissolve everything that ever made up a me – permanently.

75

The assembly hall is loud with all the classes in my year and the one above.

– Come on, children, assembly will begin – take your seats please.

– Where are you going for your holidays?

It's a girl with sun-kissed skin and blonde hair and I don't even bother trying to answer as she chats about how her family are all taking a trip to Florida and I nod and don't say a fucking thing. Just trying to breathe. Trying to not clench my fists. There are too many people in here. The lights are too bright – I wish I could wear sunglasses everywhere – even to bed.

– What? I say eventually.

– What are you doing in the holidays, Jenni?

– Dunno.

What I am actually doing is going to the estate where I lived in a battered women's hostel but this time it is on a short-term placement because my entire foster family are going to France but nobody thinks it's a good idea to let me visit another country. School trips are like that too. They just say – I am not fit to represent the school. It's so funny cos I never did anything at school. I mean get high and sell stuff but that's nowhere near the school but I've never smashed anything or sworn at a teacher or even been fucking rude.

Nobody wants to take me anywhere.

– Oh.

– Aye.

– See ya then.

– Bye.

My foster siblings who are quite fucking funny to be fair have been slagging me off all week. *Have a nice time then, Jenni, send us a postcard, ay?* I like the family that I am living with a lot but they have a ton of kids and on special occasions (like at Christmas) I don't always get my care allowance, or sometimes I don't get my clothes allowance because even that is all at their discretion it turns out, and they like me, like they really do, but they will kick me out soon anyway and they will go on their holiday and I will just be this fuck-up that nobody really treats normal, like a government-sponsored lodger you don't want to sit on a beach with or go for a nice meal or something.

I've decided to take a job working in a chip shop instead of dealing. I start on Thursday at teatime and finish late. Fridays will be a chore at school but it's enough cash to keep me in cigarettes. I took the books I borrowed back to the library. I can't focus lately to read. I chat with my friends at school but I feel so fucking far away from everything. We all file into history class. Take our tables. The teacher is looking excited to see me. Each person gets feedback – discusses their project – I picked the suffragettes.

– I have to say, in front of the whole class, you are the best young historian I have ever taught in thirty years, Jenni.

– Thank you.

Take my assignment off her table and there aren't even any glances cos I'm not even vaguely considered a swot any more.

76

The girl with the brown eyes is in this weird safe house, living with a psychopathic bitch, whose old man is in prison. The woman is away though – so we get ready together all excited, we're going to meet one of her pals first and get some speed bombs.

– Her fiancé just died so she needs a night out.

– That's so sad! How did he die?

– HIV.

– Fuck, she must be devastated.

– Aye, dinnae mention it, the virus is all over Edinburgh the now, ay, like literally, and also, dinnae mention that VCR I sold – cos I chored it from someone she knows, ay?

– Okay. Where does she stay?

– Pilton.

The girl with the brown eyes has got all her gold rings on, necklaces, tight trousers, she takes her trip and I take mine, then we head to another estate miles away, the bus goes by a really dingy wee bit of harbour and industrial estates and then we're on it for ages before we jump off at a wee warren of blocks of flats that all look the same – it's a lot worse than the council area I live in, not worse than the one I have the short-term placement coming up in though. Her pal is much older than us, a tiny wee thing, blonde hair, really nice, speeding off her tits, and as we leave her flat she grabs her lipstick and a cosh with spikes on it and puts them in her handbag.

– Just in case, ay.

– Aye, we getting a taxi?

– Aye!

I guess that's a way for a lassie to stay safe right enough. Her cosh has a long chain, to swing and take someone out. By the time we get to the club we have come up hard! My friend has been hanging out with skinheads here, they're not there when we arrive though, and my speed bomb kicks in with the trip and smoke and I knock back Jack Daniel's and Cokes and I feel fucking spectacular now – like I radiate light.

I feel like nobody has ever harmed me.

Up on the dance floor.

Pretty red lights bop across the floor below me.

I'm wearing bell-bottom jeans and a T-shirt and dancing to 'Sweet Child o' Mine' when a guy with long hair comes up and lies down on the floor in front of me playing air guitar and the whole bar is watching and it is funny and stupid and I am so high that – for a second – I feel totally free.

– Babe, I need to leave, I'm having a bad trip, I'll see you later, right?

Her brown eyes are like long haunted tunnels.

– Are you sure? I'll come back.

– No, stay out, I'll be fine.

Then her pal is chewing gum like fuck and saying we'll have a great night, pats her bag with her pet weapon so I know we will be okay, and while I've been dancing she's made pals with a guy called Freddie, wee mental guy from the other estate too, and he's funny, I like him, and then a posh guy with a puffa coat latches on to our group and he's like an MSP or something and we all know he is buying us drinks because he is after me. I'm not scared, nobody here will let him do a thing to me. The girl and Freddie are using me as bait. All I want to do is dance. Then the club is shut and we go up to the posh guy's flat and the walls are all chequered, black and white – they have literally put squares up all over it – and his flatmate is shouting at me.

– Do you fucking know what people like him would do to someone like you?

– Aye, I fucking do, actually.

Freddie nods towards the front door and as I get up and go through it she stands up and takes the cosh out and begins swinging it like fuck – posh cunts scatter! We are already out the front door when the MSP guy runs after us to come too – we get a taxi to Freddie's auntie's house and she answers in her nightie having just been woken up by us.

– You robbing wee cunt, you turned my flat over, yer no welcome here!

– Sorry! I uhm, I'm fucking sorry!

She slams the door. We are all off again and this time it is the last-chance 5 a.m. saloon – his grandad's flat.

It is tiny.

Stinks.

Cigarettes and tinned tomato soup and crone.

He plays country and western music.

The walls are flowery.

Each curtain is a different pattern of flowers. The sofa has a swirly pattern. The floor is a big orange-and-brown pattern that whorls. The posh guy sits on the edge of the sofa trying to look totally easy with all of this and the girl is dancing away having her best night out in ages and Freddie's grandad cracks open a lager.

– Pub opens just after 6 a.m., he says.

– That's early! I say.

– Has tae be open first thing, Jenni! You are coming, ay?

– Aye!

I am totally up for going to the pub if it means I get out of this floral fucking nightmare, it's lucky the acid wore off before the speed. We get our shit together and traipse down the stairwell and it is light outside. People with jobs and lives are just getting up to go for their first pee, while we all walk into a bar with no windows. It's a concrete drinking box. 6.01 a.m. Big scabby door, a pool table, jukebox – we go in and order White Russians and rack up balls on the pool table. I can't believe how busy it is in here for early as fuck, there must be twenty guys already drinking.

Freddie is after me to turn the posh guy over for money.

– I'm not fucking anyone.

– No, you don't need to, just say if he doesn't give you his coat then you'll say he tried to touch you.

– No.

– Come on, you look like a fucking angel, we could make so much money!

– No.

– His coat is worth about a fucking grand, Jenni, just get that off him then.

– No.

– You're killing me, you could hustle the fucking Pope and get away with it, look at you, you're just such a fucking lovely lassie, Jenni, please, we can go in together, like Bonnie and Clyde but you know, radger!

– No, I don't care if he's rich or not, I don't want anyone's stuff, look, I'm away!

– Fuck's sake!

I say bye to the woman and she sits happy as a cosh owner in the middle of a three-day binge while the posh guy is gutted I'm heading out of reach and Freddie follows me right onto the bus – where we sit among morning commuters and I light a cigarette and they all sit in office uniforms giving me dirty looks but too scared to say anything because we are both clearly still fucked up. Eventually Freddie gives up trying and gets off the bus. I go up to the safe house to see the girl with brown eyes. Do the secret buzz. She answers the door and I'm taken into the living room to smile and pretend to be her wee sister – and there are five men in there and they nod – return to talking – and each of them has a gun, just casually, sat at their feet.

– It's better you don't hear anything they're talking about, the girl with the brown eyes says in the hall all quiet.

– Okay.

– Come on, into the kitchen.

She has me in there with the door shut and the radio on and I get stoned and think I better concoct some kind of a story for my foster parents about what I did at my friend's house last night. I'll say we got a vegetarian pizza maybe. Then we did our homework, and then we watched a film.

77

I am at the back of the bike sheds. It is Easter so I am tripping for Jesus. I just have to meet one last person then I can go to the beach with some new friends – I'm hanging out with a girl from school who is like my own age! She's becoming a good friend. I really like her. We are heading out with a couple of older guys but they're nice, it's okay. I am trying to do things that are normal. I was with a guy for a while who made me feel so loved then someone stabbed him in his leg right down to the bone and chopped part of his ear off and one night another bunch of guys stopped in a car to ask if I was his bird and I had to say no cos he'd told me if they knew I was his girl-friend they'd rape me just to get to him and now he won't speak to me any more. His dealer did heroin with him but only on a Wednesday and (as dealers always seem to be) he was wanting all over me. The guy I was with told him not to even think it. It was nice. Feeling protected for a minute. Like some-body noticed, and gave a fuck. Anyway, that's all over and now I'm going out with someone else.

– How many tabs do you want? I ask the guy who's just turned up and he counts out his money.

– I'll take whatever you have left, Jenni, ta.

– Here you go.

I hand all the wee LSD squares over and the guy who asked me to get him some trips unfolds the half-sheet of ohm tabs and then – he takes the entire lot, in one go.

– What? he says, shrugging at me!

– Are you going to be okay?

– Fuck aye, I need at least that much for a decent trip these days.

I feel very bad now. I am a bad minor dealer. What if he flips out and doesn't make it back and it's because I sold him enough LSD for a football team?

– Can ye get me more, Jenni?

– Noh. I think I might stop dealing, actually.

– That's a shame.

– Where are you going, anyway – fir your trip?

– YMCA disco!

That's what he says.

Ten trips!

YMCA fucking disco!

He motors off pretty fucking happy.

I'm avoiding the top flats and trying to stay away from that whole area cos the pimp keeps sending guys out looking for me. I'll be walking along the street and some gadge will just fall in step and try to get me to go up to the flat – so, I hate it.

We drive out to the beach.

I roll a thirty-skin joint while tripping and watching the lights across the water.

It's so pretty to look at.

Soothes me.

78

I am staying with a couple in a tiny wee council flat, not far from Freddie's grandad. I hope I don't fucking bump into him. The social worker drops me off after informing me there are no other names for me unless I pick one. I think about calling myself Star but my identity is so fucking tenuous after all these places I think I'll just have to pick something normal. My usual foster family are in France getting tans and eating nice food and swimming in the sea while I am in a six-by-four block of council flats, but the woman is nice and so is her husband and they have a permanent foster kid and she comes in and it turns out it is the one who gave me the wooden Buddha in the old kids' home, so that is quite funny!

Everything that could go wrong does.

I end my 'holiday' at six stone with chapped lips and no sleep having had several nights in the cells and someone threatening to kneecap me – and this family taking me back again.

– Why are you letting me come back?

– You look like our daughter did, just before she died on heroin.

In the bathroom there is a tiny girl with a big head and a concave face. Truthfully, I've been doing this to forget all the things I could not take. Too much of it! I got in trouble with some horrible woman too who now says she is going to batter me when she sees me and it's because she wants a reputation and her scummy neighbour stole off her and blamed it on me and what these parents see is that I am literally still a kid, but I am so far gone I don't even know if it is possible to make it back again and nobody else seems to know either.

79

I see her in a shopping centre weeks later. It is a shit mall. They called it a mall cos everyone is trying to be American lately. It looks like a black spaceship with a thin red line around it. I only go in there to get hair bobbles from Claire's Accessories. The woman is browsing at some window with her gnarly wee sidekick. I know a fight is going to happen one way or another – so I may as well call it now.

– Alright.

– Alright?

– I heard you wanted to see me – we should go up the park and talk it out.

I nod towards the back entrance and the park behind it and they look at each other, both slightly unnerved.

– You've got fucking balls, coming over to say that to me, she says.

We walk out.

The park is bright and it is getting cold. It's that time of year again. Things turning to ochre and gold, I love autumn more than any season really. There is a thing I realised lately. If the anger from my entire life and everything that happened to me ever really got out it would kill somebody. Like if I really let it out properly. The only thing I am scared of really now – is me. As we slow down to pick a spot I prepare myself, in my head – I say the words to myself over and over and over – no matter what, don't unlock the box or someone is leaving here dead.

I don't give a fuck what happens to me.

That's clear I suppose!

– I don't believe in violence, it's fucking stupid, I say.

The two of them look at me like I have a full-on fucking head of horns.

– You took E's from my flat!

– Did I fuck, you know I didn't, you fucking know it! That isnae what this is about, this is about you wanting to batter a girl from care so you can get a reputation for being hard ...

She is twice as heavy as me, huge feet, a lot fucking older, and I know she is summoning up bad fucking memories from her childhood to take that pain out on me so maybe I can carry it away – I know far too often how others have been hurt, I feel it and can see the ways it destroys them.

Fingers grab into each other's hair.

We yank each other's heads locked in, going around in circles, and all I want to do – is make sure I don't hurt her.

It's fucked up I know!

Despite how much bigger she is than me, she can't get me onto the ground.

I feel the edges of my temper like blood at the back of my mouth.

Attacks of rage so severe when I was a wee girl that I'd become totally immobilised.

Her pal takes a full run at me then and the two of them get me on the ground.

She kicks me full force, big massive feet straight into my bony wee face – again, and again – they tear clumps of my hair out and smash my face off the kerb again and again, then stand back so they can get a run to kick me – in the head – there is white noise and I am still holding on to my rage until she leans over ...

– I'm going to break your finger now, she says.

She tries to grab a hold of it.

That's how I write …

I've never broken a bone in my fucking life.

Through one blood-red eye (other is already swollen shut) I turn to look at her, I roar – a noise comes out of me so fucking primal and loud that all the trees stop rustling their leaves and grass becomes as brittle as shards of glass and they both falter and begin to back away from me fast … even though I am still on the deck, they look scared and they should because if I have to levitate upright and put her down at this point I will do it and nobody will stop me.

In my whole life I never heard that sound.

There is something under my voice and woven intricately through it, something of my humanity, but there is also a clear note that I have always known – there are worse things than blood and flesh.

I've died countless times already.

Started my life playing with monsters and the dead who couldn't leave the hospital.

There is far worse than dying and I have done that too.

I pick myself up off the ground.

Brush myself off and run home – blood everywhere – both eyes nearly totally closed – passers-by shrink away from me as I think cold and clean – at least I know if I have to do it, I can take a kick in, and I didn't hurt anyone I wouldn't do time for.

It is a long way back through the council estate – my foster folks are back now, from their holiday, and I hammer on the door and she screams …

– What have they done to you?!

Limp upstairs, bits of hair fall out in my hands, blood is everywhere.

– Call the polis, call the fucking police!

Spit blood into the sink in the bathroom and look up to
check I still have all my teeth. Bare them. That's how you
smile. Like this. Fucking idiots! They think this kind of shit
fucking hurts me?

– Don't call the police, I won't fucking talk to them, it'll
only make it worse.

There is noise and movement outside the bathroom door.

I am unrecognisable.

Dab myself.

Nose spread across my face.

Lip bloody and one eye completely swollen shut already, the
other a tiny slit of pure red. Where the whites and blues of my
eyes should be there is only swollen bloody blackened skin.
Clumps of hair and blood swirl down the drain, a long open
scar runs up into my hairline. Into the shower, then pyjamas,
then the back garden to sit peering through a wee dash of red
light and refusing to speak to anyone.

– If you won't talk to the police, you'll have to talk to Scooter.

– How?

– Because we are not leaving you like this …

My foster mother is teary. I nod as her eldest son, who's
done time, who I don't know that well, who has great taste in
music, and is a scooter boy and has always been nice as fuck to
me – well, he turns up. Strides into the garden where I am bal-
ancing sunglasses on a pulped face. He gently takes them off.
Sits. Lights a roll-up, hands me one too, he makes prison ones,
super skinny.

– Tell me everything. The whole fucking lot. All of it.

It's not a request.

80

My foster parents watch from the house. I make sure to not tell him all of the things – not stuff that will put anyone in jail, or have anyone killed. I don't tell him about the pimp. I don't tell him about the safe house. I do tell him about the woman and her flat and her neighbour taking her stuff when we were made to go to the cells.

– You won't go up there again.

– The high-rises?

– No, that's the last time you score there, it's done, you stay the fuck away from all of them.

Nod.

Go to bed.

Sometimes even someone I don't know that well does something huge to stand up for me and it reminds me how many good people there are and no matter how many horrible ones I meet I choose to never forget that, he didn't need to care but he did. I am grateful. It means another way has to be found, for me, I can't just keep going up there and getting high and I needed someone to make that choice for me because I say I will stop taking stuff and I don't, I just get even more high and I hate it.

I sleep on my back with the taste of blood in my mouth.

81

The prostitutes from further up her building threatened that woman from the bottom flats with a knife and told her to leave little girls alone and stop bragging about picking on them. It makes me want to cry because they barely even knew me but were just so fucking nice to me. Then Scooter's fiancée tells the woman to leave me alone as well, cos she is saying to people she is going to batter me again. My foster brother's fiancée was like – she's a kid, she's literally half the size of you! Then the girl with the brown eyes was in the loos at a club with all the skinheads and heard the two women bragging about this girl they'd pulped, so – she put her up against the wall and said it was her little sister they were fucking with and she better not look at me again.

I am jumpy.

Everywhere I go.

The pimp still keeps sending the same guy to find me too. He has curly hair and is skinny and I'll be walking and he just falls into step next to me. He tells me how much the guy wants me to go back up to his high-rise and how much he misses talking to me and how nothing will happen if I go up there and I just keep walking until he gives up. If I go anywhere near that flat something so bad is going to happen to me.

– Morning!

– It is, aye.

– So, what's it going to be then, Jenni?

My foster dad is sat on the sofa smiling. He gives me a fag. I like the foster dad here, he has a great face, lived in, so does the foster mum, they are good people and funny, and a new social worker has been already to talk about whether I will get moved on from here but we all know I will. I don't blame them. I'm always going missing. The other kids act up then cos if I can get away with it why can't they get away with more?

– Just send me to a kids' home, it's honestly fine.

He smiles.

– You leaving here will be the hardest kid for her to watch go …

Nods towards his wife in the kitchen.

– I know.

– You are going to be only one of two things when you grow up, as I see it, Jenni.

– What's that?

– You will either be the first person in this family to go all the way to the top in education, you'll be the first one who has passed through this house to get a degree, go all the way to the top in your profession, or …

– What?

I light a cigarette, drag deep, my face is better now but my eyes are still bruised so I've taken to wearing sunglasses from 8 a.m. until bedtime, but I've dressed myself nice, black polo neck, black leggings, black Doc boots, I am waiting for the girl with the brown eyes to call because she has rematerialised from fuck knows where.

– Or, you will be the first major female drugs baron in Europe.

I grin.

– It's good to know you have faith in me.

– It's only going to be one of the two.

– You think?

– Whatever you do, you won't stop until you are the best one out there doing it.

– Might be a long road …

– Aye.

The phone rings and it is so good to hear my pal's voice and I am out the door, up to the bus stop, then into town. I meet her outside Waverley where we used to skive off school together when we were in the kids' unit. We used to joke about owning the Castle one day. She has shaved her hair off and has a wee fringe and a dark khaki bomber jacket, skinny black jeans, bovver boots – she lifts my sunglasses up and whistles.

– Better tell me all about it, ay?

– Aye!

We go down in the glass lift – look down at the bright food forecourt. The water fountains have pennies in them where people throw wishes. Kids stick their hands in the water to steal them. I'll nip into the Body Shop when we leave. I wear White Musk perfume a lot, or jojoba oil. I'll get a lip balm too. I am trying to take care of myself lately in some kind of a way. I am going vegetarian again. I have been thinking when I get older maybe I could get a job working in human rights or something. Do something actually useful with my life. We order from the burger place, just a coffee for each of us.

I take an empty red metallic tin ashtray from another table.

– Okay, Jenni, I've got some stuff to tell you and I need you to be open-minded, just like, listen to me, but you go first.

She can see that I'm not the person I was just a few months before. Her face changes as I go on but I don't tell her about the guy, or the other ones, because I am scared of what he'll do if I say anything. I feel like the only way to be safe on that one is to stay quiet. I tell her all the rest of it though.

– Fucking hell!

– I know.

– Well, you are going to have to go and batter the bird then, I mean you need to kick her fucking cunt in – like properly!

– I don't want to.

– You don't have a fucking choice!

She looks at me levelly and her eyes are so brown and pretty, her skin is paler lately so her freckles stand out more and she suits them and it is so good to see her face. I remember us both laughing so much that Christmas she stayed in the kids' home with me.

– So, what did you want to tell me?

– You'll just listen, Jenni?

– Aye.

– No judging …

– I would never, ever fucking judge you for anything, I know you!

She is shaky so I still myself to try and calm her.

– I started staying with this woman in Leith, ay, she was taking me out partying, ended up I got in debt with it, and then she said there was an easy way to pay it off …

Her hands tremble.

– Aye?

– Just get in a car, ay, quick, hand jobs mostly, then blow jobs. Thing that's so bad about it, is it's so easy. Once you've done it once, you know you can do it again. You ever fight with hookers in their forties on the docks? Seriously! Once you've learned to fight with them you can fucking annihilate anyone.

– I don't like the idea of you having to let anyone touch you!

– I know.

Tears. Both of us, blinking, people bustling around, regular glances at my black eyes, one still fairly closed up. I get us two more coffees. I am thinking all the while, can hear the milk-shake machine and some kid crying for fries because they dropped them, and a security guard looks over the forecourt to see if any of the usual shoplifters are in and behind us the regular swoosh and burst of cold as people go out the doors and up to the train station steps. I wish I could put us both on a train right now and never come back to this shitty town again. I'm also thinking about how to get high again – to just not be feeling because the memories lately ... just won't go away!

– What if I did it?

I drop a third brown sugar into my coffee and tip in two creamer pots and she shakes her head, vehemently.

– Don't you dare even fucking think of it, Jenni!

– How? It's okay fir you but it isnae alright fir me?

– Aye.

– I don't think so!

She leans forward and looks into my eyes.

– You wouldn't survive it, you've already been through ... way, way too much, you are sensitive as hell, and you'd snap, sooner or later. Some people are built to be able to learn how to handle it at least a bit and you are not, you'd end up ... I don't know.

We drink in silence for a while.

I find it so hard to have men's hands on my skin half the time as it is.

Usually lie there with clenched fists and a clamped jaw and utter rage in my body and none of them ever fucking notice. Even the ones I've gone out with. I hate it. That feeling goes so far back in me. She is totally right and we both know it. I stay high because there is a train going five hundred miles an hour next to me at all times and on every carriage there is a memory I can't bear.

– I was so nervous to tell you, Jenni, I was worried you wouldn't want to be friends with me.

– Are you kidding? You are the nicest girl I know, there is literally nothing that will ever make me feel any different, but you know I hate that fucking woman for pulling you into that, I really, really fucking hate her!

– What else was I going to do? I've no money, crashing at the safe house again, no flat, adopted parents won't speak to me, my own mum ... well, she's been doing this kind of work forever, there isn't anywhere fir me to go.

– I'm going to ask my foster parents if you can come and stay with us.

– I doubt it!

– I'll beg them.

– We better go, I need to get back – will you come back up there with me?

– Aye. Funny thing happened though, well, no really, I went back up the flats to score and nobody will sell to me, my foster brother went up and apparently warned them all that he'd break their fucking arms if they sold me fucking anything, so I'm cut off, do you know what I was thinking, this is crazy right, but what if ah hung out with pals ma own age? Like, what if I joined a group and like tried tae write or something?

– Write what?

– Ah dih ken, like a play!

– I've no fucking idea what you are talking about, Jenni.

82

I have a note in my diary that reads – *Dear future, if you are reading this, then a word to the undead from the see ya's and long gone's, be beautiful, this gift ... life.*

I'm at an all-night rave.

Outfit like this: Cinderella shoes, platform soles (wood), metal round nails as feature to hold top bit of leather on (dull bronze), tights to cover my pale legs, velvet hot pants with a high waist, tight white T-shirt, little black waistcoat, black velvet choker, hair is bobbed and dyed extra bright copper, it is shiny and smooth, no lipstick, never wear it but I've done cat's eyes with liner, nails painted red, we have E's and speed and it's folk from school, well, one, and the guys we've been hanging out with. I floated in here with ecstasy lining my bra cos it's the easiest way to get it in. A whole city of neon lights bounce and a sea of hands all raised in the air – fingertips reaching up to touch the lights – lasers, scanning over the crowd – I know that light – I know that shine – if you asked me what I was doing here right now I'd say I was looking for God – love – all around me whorling balletic dancers lifting the music – whoop, whoop! Pound our feet against the ground and whoooop, whooooop! The calls come from deep down where cave people used to dance like this – belonging – connection – it is like nothing any of us have felt out there because there is just total love in here – so much of it – people look at strangers with pure fucking joy in their heart. I am up on a speaker – words lilt up – I need ... (the crowd lifts visibly) your loving … (howls) and I know what is coming and there are tears on my face because – everybody does need love.

Even me.

This life has been so fucking intense already and I am so fucking grateful for these moments, to know there is a part of me that is always whole, tapped into the cosmos, looking towards the light, the shine, the God source – female as she is – like some goblins told an ootlin all about – that first light – big bang – a force of energy radiating out for 13.9 billion years and I can see it across the light on the fingertips of everyone in this room – fucking hell, it shines!

83

Sometimes people are beautiful. Kind and hopeful and giving and good and not doing things just to gain. I want to be one of those ones. Just like I did as a wee girl totally in love with fairy tales. I don't want to be bitter. I've met people so bitter they can skin you with a sentence. I have to let so much go. Too many things have happened to me. I think about every door I walked through, how many of those things that happened were anything to do with me and how many were just to do with other people?

– Jenni, it's the phone!!

– OOOKAYYY. Alright?

– Aye. Well, no, Jenni, I need you to speak to me every day for the next seven days, okay?

It's the girl with the brown eyes and she is jittery. Picture her at the docks, taking car numbers so she can call the police if another girl is not back in half an hour. She is phoning from the safe house. My foster mother has a look on her face because she hates me talking to the girl with the brown eyes. I asked them if they'd take her in for a few weeks so she wouldn't have to go back on the game again and they said no. Their other kids rush through the kitchen and the dogs start barking.

– Okay, I will.

– You promise?

– Yes.

I hang up.

It's the last time I ever hear her voice.

84

Some boys from my year at school are counting out money and laughing. They all straighten up and look awkward when they see me.

– What are youz doing?

– Nothing!

– Taking bets, another one adds.

– About what?

They all go quiet.

– About whether you are going to make it to sixteen or not, one says.

– I see.

Don't say anything, just go up the street cos the girls have asked me to go out and drink with them tonight and so I am trying to be like other people my age, we're all going to hang out at the car park behind Tesco, get pissed, have a laugh, there's a rumour going about that one of the hardest girls in care is going to be there tonight, I know her by reputation, we've travelled through the same kids' homes and units at different times and all the girls at school who live in nice houses with their families (some have problems but most of them fucking don't) have been stirring the pot saying me and this girl are going to fight and I really hope not because I know I don't have it in me to lie down and play dead again so if we did fight it would be carnage. I'm fairly certain she's harder than me so I wouldn't be able to not lose my temper or I'd get pulped. It makes me feel tired just thinking about it. I walk by the charity shop and there is a dictionary in the window. I remember when I was actually trying to learn every word in it.

Later on there's about thirty of us all hanging around within an hour or so, all girls, all drinking, all from different schools and places, loud and laughing and shouting and goading and making jokes, and the other girl from care is over on that side and I am over on this one. Then it's time for us to front up to each other. I put my hand up to the circle of girls around us both.

– Stay fucking back, it's just me and her.

They do, gladly.

She walks into the circle and I meet her in the middle.

We're surrounded by little jeers and a bloodlust … to hear teeth crack and see skin split, we both feel it radiating off them, groups of girls who grew up together, lived on the same streets, whose brothers know each other, whose uncles and aunts help their parents out, who go on holidays together or have birthday parties, who get Christmas presents that they don't have to buy for their-fucking-selves, and all they really, really, really – fucking want to see tonight is the hardest girls from care kick fuck out of each other for their own mindless entertainment.

– Alright? I say.

– Alright!

She's taller than me, wee bit bigger, we don't smile.

– The way I see it is this … I say.

The group around us crane their necks to try and hear what we are saying but I am talking quiet enough for just us to hear, because what I have to say is nobody else's fucking business.

– Aye, Jenni?

– If you want to fight me I will, you want to fight – we can do it, it's fine, I'll fucking fight you, aye?

– Aye, she nods.

– But this circle standing around us, all these nice wee lassies, every single one of them is going to go home tonight to their nice mummies and daddies and their wee decorated bedrooms and the rest of their family, and their security, and their happy wee fucking lives, and we – are not.

– Aye, I know.

– So, if you want to be the entertainment – a wee buzz for all these fucking cunts (and that's all it will be – a cheap thrill for them before they go home) – then I'll do it, I'll fucking fight you but not one of them knows what it is like – for me, or you – and they don't even fucking want to because we are not like them, and we will never fucking be like them, and they don't get it for even one fucking second, they don't go through what you or me do and they don't know what that means at all, but if you want to put on a free show for them, at our expense, then go for it.

The girls are straining, calling things out, wary enough though to keep back from both of us. My heart is fucking battering off my chest. I'm ready for it to turn. I look at her and she looks at me. I know she catches it – it's a glint, and somehow I know just like she does without saying a word to each other, something none of these girls do, something none of them are ever going to fucking see or understand for their whole long fucking lives.

She puts her hand out and shakes mine and pats me on the arm.

– I'd never fucking fight you, she says.

– You too …

If it wasn't for all the arseholes around us I'd have hugged her. We have both acknowledged something and we go back to our own corners with dignity and clear fucking sight. If these girls want a boxing ring – they can get their own fucking hair pulled out. I want to keep what is left of mine. I like that girl as well. I know she has about as much fucking chance as I do, of being okay, of surviving this, we all know it by this age, how many kids from care we know who are dead, in prison, on the game, junkied, mental. Our chances are slim as a crack of light through a distant door – and what we don't need to ever fucking do is fight each other. Even fucking less for entertainment – because what we are living through is not a thrill, it's not a story, it's not a buzz, it's not a joke, it's not gossip, it is not a story that other people tell, it's not words on a file or spoken in the kids' court, it is a dense thud of silence when we walk in a room, it is not a bet someone will ever win, it's ambulance doors swallowing me overdosed at twelve years old and ready to die because of what I have already lived through – it is real – we are trying to survive the unsurvivable and none of it is stacked in our favour and it is all totally against us.

I have all respect for the girl.

To even still be standing!

I think she is fucking amazing to have made it through this far at all, and as she walks away with her group, in my head I wish her only fucking well with every-single-thing!

I go to the phone box and ring the safe-house number once more.

It is dead.

No answerphone.

Nothing.

I know in my heart that I won't ever see the girl with the brown eyes again. And I know this too. She saved me. More than once! From going down a road I would not have been able to come back from. I couldn't do it for her though and I hate it. One of the girls was asking earlier if I was ready for our exams coming up. It's not possible to study in a kids' home. I won't even sit them.

85

He gives me a penguin trip. I feel weird about the way he is looking at me, something is going on with this dealer, can feel it, then my ex walks in – the one I split up with on acid because I thought a guy who knew him was trying to get him to take me upstairs so he could shag me and it was giving me brutal flashbacks.

Other things!

Too many!

A boyfriend who punched every lamp post on the hill one night and broke his knuckles. How I've had more lines crossed than I could ever write down. Right now though I'm tripping so hard it's like I took fifty trips … wonder if his dealer pal has given me a triple dose? Go into the bathroom and look in the mirror.

I.

Don't.

Know.

Who.

I am.

I don't know who I am!

I don't know – who I am!

I totally don't!

Peer at this girl in the mirror who happens to be me and I have no idea who I am!

I don't know who I am.

I don't know who I am!

I'm the demon. Cos I dumped a guy while tripping? Cos I've been fucked over so many fucking times and I am so fucking scared of it happening to me again? He knew that! I'm out the door. Running! Right across a busy road. Cars beep and someone shouts. I'm right onto a bus and sitting down and the light is bright, so bright! I can hear thoughts in people's heads. I can just dip right into their head and back out! It's so easy! Telepathy! Just like I had always hoped as a little kid. It is terrifying because I could just step out of my body entirely. Grip onto the bus rail. It is cold and silver and all the rails begin to fly by in tracers behind me. I don't remember my name. I don't! I don't know who I am. I don't know what is going on! I must have had so much fucking acid. I think he spiked me. I need to get off the bus! I need to find my way back to the new kids' home. I can't remember the route. I see the cheap shitty shopping mall all black with a red light around it like a spaceship and I leap, clang the bell, race down the steps, I hit the ground running, anger is rolling off my body – actually rolling down off my body and along the road in front of me.

I'm going to kill someone, or die.

I'd rather commit suicide than hurt someone else, that is the deal I made with myself way back when they made me believe I was the monster, my adopted mum writing me notes saying she'd still speak to me if I grew up to be a murderer (I was about eight), and the mistrust in people's eyes soon as they hear you are from care and the police closing cell doors and the guys whose heads would prick up when they heard – you are from care?

You are not owned?

Nobody is going to come looking for you, no?

They might for some kids in care who have happy lives somewhere but that is not how it has been for me.

Run towards a bus stop.

It's all gone too far, I've snapped!

Fear rolls off me and down the dark wet street like thunder.

I am by a roundabout where I used to sleep rough when I was like thirteen, hoody pulled up over my head and breathing into it to try and stay warm, and there is a graveyard nearby I slept in once or twice too and there is a car garage forecourt all dark and shiny with its signs in the windows in red and I am going to have to kill myself when the next car comes because this is too much, I need to just jump, fast enough to end it!

No choice!

My life has made me terrified, of me!

First car …

Step out towards it and then another voice, somewhere way back inside me, tells me to hold on because something in my future is going to need me, and it won't end like this, I didn't survive everything to die now, and I need to get through this – a psychotic break on LSD – drug psychosis – get back to the unit and tell the staff and go to the psych ward where I always knew I would end up.

86

Outside the window every single thing is identical. It's like we are running past the same film set over and over, so how do I know when to get off? I can't remember where the new kids' unit is! Then – finally – a break, a field, a bus stop, me bouncing off the bus through a crowd of kids and one saying – did you see her eyes? – and me striding to the unit with anger rolling away from my body in every direction.

All the memories I tried to forget are in technicolour. A little girl – no voice – taken out of bed, walked down that hallway, and what she did, what she did! Even further back. I am in other rooms. Mouth full. Blacking out. My little-kid body covered in scabies, weeping infected sores. My second adopted mother – hit, too hard this time, scour out the shine, not one single second of sympathy for seven years. Sleeping in doorways. Washing myself in the river and lying down, in the dark, my face looking out from a newspaper, why did nobody who saw me – stop me living in the woods at twelve years old?

Dark roads …

A bare hallway in the high-rise, the colours, zip, anger rolls off my body from all the way back on a Victorian psychiatric hospital – and all this time my monsters have been swimming around the ward, lonely and waiting for me to go home.

87

I can't make eye contact with anyone. A girl who is brittle jaggy and stole my shoes goes to get into my face then shrinks back quickly. All the kids in the unit instinctively know to stay the fuck away from me right now. I go to the office door. It's the member of staff I like least. He speaks French and has a mullet and round spectacles. He looks at us like we are vile little specimens he'd like to cut open with a fine scalpel.

Close the office door behind me, I need to say it quickly.

– How was your night?

– Bad. I have had a psychotic break on LSD and I need to go to a hospital – now!

He takes in my demeanour, trying to conceal his intrigue.

– Sit down, tell me more.

– I can't sit down! I've had LSD tonight but I have tripped a hundred times and never felt anything like this, I need to be locked up, I can't remember … I'm just, I'm losing … I am …

Unable to breathe.

He is getting car keys then, a light jacket; kids have been silenced at the TV area.

Some other member of staff is to look after them.

We walk out.

Click on a seat belt in his car.

Can feel his intellectual brain trying to take control, to keep himself superior – to this, to me – he asks me questions only just trying to conceal the mocking …

Stare back at him.

A big lump in his throat as he swallows. His face registering, I am really too far gone for these kinds of games. He asks me stuff then from really far away …

– What is your name?

I know this one.

There is a name somewhere …

Rifle through these old papers in my mind, I could pick one of four – which is the right one?

Maybe none really belong to me.

Finally land on the latest one and it is such a relief to haul it up from the depths like a rotten bit of fish and profess it from my mouth – like a spell.

– My name is Jenni.

– What is your last name?

It's a long journey down through the echoing chambers – time elongates and he is beginning to panic just around the edges …

– Fagan, it is Jenni Fagan.

– Do you know what year it is?

So it goes, all the way into town, to the hospital, not the kids' one this time, they don't need to see this kind of shit. The staff member hands me sliced oranges in the hospital emergency waiting room – as he gives my details. I heard that vitamin C can bring you down. The nurses bustle around. It won't be long now. They will put me into a padded room and stick a needle in so it can all be over. I can stop trying to stay sane. It's so tiring. I can just leave my body for good this last final time … it has always been coming.

I have hung in!

– They'll see us in a few minutes, I just want to ask you something, before you go in, Jenni.

– What?

– If you are unable to come back from this, would you be willing to be used as an example – to other teenagers – about why you should never take LSD?

– What?

I am not coming back.

They can do what they want with me.

This man kind of smirks, then, right at me.

I go into a little white cubicle and fear rolls off down the hallways – looking for a host – they really must restrain it!

– Hello, so, what can we do for you tonight, Jenni?

– I've lost my mind.

– How do you know?

– I just do, I've taken LSD but it has never been like this before.

– What do you want us to do?

I can't believe he even needs to ask me.

– Lock me up!

– Where?

– In a little padded room.

– I see. We can't do that, it seems you are having a really bad reaction to drugs but you will come back down, and then you'll need to see how you feel in the morning. You just need to go home and let it wear off.

I am so – shocked.

I can't believe this level of insanity is going to have to be survived on my own, like everything fucking else!

88

Once an hour the night nurse comes to my bedroom door.

I am ready and waiting.

Knock.

Knock.

Knock.

She chaps three times to check I'm still alive and that I've not peeled my skin off.

Isn't three times the way demons knock?

Stand right behind the door and open it and we are almost nose-to-nose.

The night nurse is pretty composed in the face of drug psychosis I have to say.

I look at her like I'm ready to go work – in an office!

Close the door.

Then it's back to counting every minute until she knocks on that door an hour later – I open the door again and look at her and she looks me over then she goes back downstairs. One time she switches it up and asks me if I might like some toast.

– No, ta.

– Is there anything you need?

– Nope.

I write twenty-five pages by the time sunrise comes.

Still here.

This is a kind of breathing.

A gilled creature above water swimming in air and nobody can see that I never knew how to breathe at all.

I am meant to go back to school after tonight.

It's my English exam this morning.

I write my way through every second of my bad trip. Document the fear, the noises, a sound of a motorbike outside that sounds like freedom, fear ripping out of my pores, never easing, I think I'm going to flip out, hurt somebody – think about all the bad thoughts I've always tried to hide, how I'd count the steps to school, avoid the cracks, make deals with myself, if I can survive just one more minute, just another after that, like obsessive thinking, like there is something wrong with me but I don't know what. I climb out onto the rooftop of the unit just as the sun comes up and floods the fields and trees with light until everything is golden yellow.

89

The shop floor is big and there are girls dotted around the room. All with multiple hoops that get smaller going up their ears. Pierced noses. One has long jet-black straight hair. I am told she is genuine Romany, travelling blood, a princess of some kind they say, she is absolutely stunning and far too cool to talk to me – that goes for most of them. There are trays of henna hair dyes, in little plastic tubs with white lids and gold writing. Red, black, yellow, blue, green. The clothes are tie-dye or lace or denim and there are patches you can buy to sew onto things. The jewellery counter has a big stand behind it where girls look down – on customers browsing through yin/yang rings.

– Just go upstairs, follow her, okay?

Nod.

Duck through a tiny creaky door and go down cold wooden steps under the belly of Edinburgh. We are at the bottom of Cockburn Street then, right under the city, going through huge rooms stacked with barrels of cheesecloth shirts from Mexico, bright coloured scarfs from India, jeans from Italy, through a warren of rooms and up a spiral staircase, up and up and up and up and up and into a tiny little turret where a skinny man with a white ponytail is surrounded by screens that show him what is going on in every single shop on the street.

– Hello.

– Hi.

– Take a seat.

– Thank you.

This is my first job interview other than drug dealing or serving chips or burning newspapers, I am nervous because this is the real world and I don't come here often. This is where people who are not in care live and this strange coked-up guy assesses me quietly.

– Where do you live?

– Out of town, it is actually a kids' home, I live in a kids' home, but I am leaving!

– Good.

– I'm going to get a little place, near here, actually, it's going to be great.

– I see, so do you have a CV or any qualifications?

– No.

– None?

– No, I had to leave school when I was fifteen – I still am, actually, fifteen.

– And why do you want to work here?

– I love clothes, adore them actually, I love things that are pretty and alternative, I love that beauty isn't just this one-dimensional thing, I love piercings and all of your shops, on the whole street, and these old tenement buildings, I mean look at them they are just – fucking amazing!

– Quite!

He grins.

– Sorry for swearing. I really want to work here, I won't be late, I need someone to, you know, just like – give me a chance really.

This is not a time to become someone who cries easily.

– I think you'd be good, I am going to put you in with this guy …

He points to a shop halfway up the street. It is Ground Control. It sells T-shirts on one side and velvet dresses and pewter and jewellery on the other side and there is a big guy called Spider who does piercings in the basement – the guy he is pointing at that I will work with is on the pewter side of the shop and he has long straight blond hair all the way down his back, skater combat long shorts, Converse, a T-shirt, chain from his keys to his belt loop, a big tattoo on his arm.

– You don't have a criminal record, anything hanging over you?

– No.

I lie sometimes.

We all do!

I'll have to go up before the kids' court soon though.

If they don't lock me up then, I won't have a record! I turn sixteen soon and my record will be wiped clean. I really, really want this job and to work on this street and so it is only a tiny lie and if it doesn't work out I can send him a postcard from Cornton Vale saying thanks for the chance! Bon voyage! His eyes are like pissholes. I'm pretty sure he is on a fuckload of coke. The different shops are all on the screen. Satanists at the top of the street selling jeans and then there is the Eden shop where the girls seem more holistic and Pie in the Sky which is more edgy and Ground Control which might be the start of a new life for me.

Just need to get through court and I should be fine to work here, if they don't lock me away. I had to put in an application to allow me to leave care as well and the outcome of my hearing will be vital to the department saying yes, I can finally leave the system.

– Can you start next week?

– Definitely.

I walk back up the street. It is a relief to not be in school any more. They asked me to leave politely. If I hadn't they would have formally expelled me. I didn't turn up for my exams. I was always anxious in school, every time I went in, I'd sit in classrooms trying not to panic and run out, every day elongated, and I am still like that whenever I go into any room I feel like I can't get out of right away, so it will be like that at work.

You can smoke in the shops when you are working though, and you can wear as many nose studs as you want, and you can doodle and swear and be well more me, I couldn't do that at school, I can watch MTV, listen to Nirvana, I know cos I went in and met the skateboarder. He has a tattoo with Straight Edge all the way down his arm and some other guy came in and started talking to him about *American Psycho* where the character fucks a woman's corpse in the eye and all the time he was smiling at me and I wondered what makes some guys so fucking pathetic and weird and creepy. In the window of the shop there was an advert for a singer in a band. I wrote down the number. It's something I always wanted to do. When I get back to the unit I phone the number. It's an Italian restaurant in town and the guy must work in the kitchen. The bass player answers after a minute and asks my age and I say I'm fifteen and I'm working in Cockburn Street and he says he'll come and meet me to go for a coffee. It's a good day all in all. I go into the living room and the young guys in the unit are wasted. Faces glowing. They look guilty when they see me.

– Where have you lot been?

– Nowhere.

– Liars.

– Fucking urnay.

– Aye, ye urr, look at the state ay ye, where ye fucking been, ya wee arseholes?

– They went to his flat again.

Stare at them, cold as I can, they all grow quiet, one is still sniggering, and I see the officer in charge of the unit take a stand at the top of the steps behind me and fold his arms and he does not say a single word when I turn around and start on them.

– Did he lock the door?

– No.

– Ye ken that is a safe house?

– Nut!

– Aye, ye ken that door is reinforced so the polis cannae fucking break it down, there are metal runners right through the walls so even with big fucking rams they'd have to take the whole building down to get through it?

– So?!

– Did he have the dogs there?

– Aye.

– Ye ken he'll fucking set them on you?

– No, he'll no, he's famous! He's in the fucking papers!

The wee one is upset now.

– He's a fucking paedo, he'll set both those fucking dogs on ye until you take your fucking trousers down and let every man in there rape you fucking senseless – you absolute – fucking – idiots! Is it worth it? Worth it to get stoned? You know what that click is gonnae sound like when they lock the fucking door on you? You only get one or two free trips there, he gave you coke, ay? E's? Did he say there will be a wee bit ketamine next time, aye?

I go after them until they are – totally straight.

I look up at the officer in charge and he nods at me, respectfully, he gets there's some things the staff can't say or do, but I can and those boys are just fucking bairns who want to act cool and each of them wishes he had a real dad that gave a fuck and instead some fancy famous paedo's going to use that to lure them into their shitty fucking world and ruin their entire fucking lives – as if they've not been through enough already.

90

I can't fold velvet dresses worth a fuck. I smoke too much. I'm good at cleaning the cabinets though. Nearly all of the staff are way older than me and friendly but also totally not and I am warned not to go to any of the parties because I am too young for orgies and satanic rituals. That's what they think! It's cute that they think I'm still a kid I guess. The guitarist from the band is coming to get me to go and audition. The bass player is a tall punk with a shaved head and he gave me a tape with all these amazing singers on it. X-Ray Spex, Lydia Lunch, Patti Smith, I've been listening to all old punk stuff, I don't listen to much else just now. Except for female blues singers. They really get to me. Bessie Smith, Sister Wynona Carr – Nina Simone is the queen though, I think so, I adore everything she ever did. I learned the songs for the band in my room in the unit. Played them over and over. The staff wished me good luck this morning. It's teatime when the guitarist and I head down Cockburn Street to his van. He has blond hair parted in the middle, down to his shoulders, and a nose hoop and I like him right away. We drive down to the docks where they have a rehearsal room. I hope for a paranoid minute that they are not going to try and have me gang-banged when I realise this is where the girl with the brown eyes used to pick up punters sometimes. We park outside a row of hut things. We go in and there is a rehearsal room with Marshall stacks on old plastic milk crates. The bass player has a Peavey PA system and there is a mic they have borrowed for me to try out. There is an upside-down cross and a huge set of tits spray-painted on the wall. They tune up. I take my shoes off.

– We'll just go for it?

– Aye.

They kick in, drum machine pressed on (they can't get a drummer who will play fast enough and the only one they did was some woman on heroin who wasn't that reliable), I take the mic like I was waiting for this moment all my life, I shout, I scream, I sing, I talk quiet, the bass and guitar fade out and they're both grinning at each other and then at me.

– Where do you live?

– I'm still in a kids' home, I'll move out really soon though, to town.

– Cool.

– That doesn't put you off?

– No.

– I hate telling people.

– It's good, you're good, you can really fucking sing, the bass player says.

Going to band practice is what I live for now.

We go to the Port of Leith pub after, and there is a cool lady who runs the place and she has blonde hair with a big bouffant and a total mishmash of people drink there. We get photographs taken down the street by my friend from high school who I've not seen for ages and he takes one with 'Failures Bought' written behind us. Our guitarist shaves his hair off for the shoot. I just wear my Doc boots and cut my hair with nail scissors. I love the songs but I want to write my own lyrics. The bass player isn't really up for me doing that though. I don't know. I guess people think you've nothing to write about when you are fifteen.

91

It's totally weird that the guitarist is going to the same night-club over in Glasgow as me tonight, and he needs E's, so I can sell him what they want. I shower in the unit, then I fill up the bath, make myself a bong, then another one, get dressed and head downstairs. My support worker is there. He is so skinny. I like his face. He told me he was in the Foreign Legion once.

– So I can still go out and stay with my pal from school?

– You can but do not get into any trouble – you have to be up before the children's court tomorrow and it is really important, okay?

– Aye.

– You promise me you will just be staying in with your pal, watching a movie, coming home?

– Brownie's honour!

– Were you in the Brownies?

– Aye. I got kicked out.

– That I can believe.

– Or maybe it was the Guides I got kicked out of, I can't remember ... a lot of stuff.

– That's trauma that does that, Jenni, it leaves a lot of blank spaces, then sometimes the memories come back, you know?

Ignore that wee bit of wisdom and take my outing money and, feeling weirdly trepidatious for some reason, head into town where Monroe meets me at the other shit shopping centre in the city (they are all crap), she looks amazing until she speaks and it is like the drugs have done something to her mind, like she is slower than she was, but I brush it off because she is so excited for later. I'm thinking about how I had to apply to be allowed to leave care for good and what would happen if they made me stay in.

– So, Jenni, there's coke, speed, E's, really, really strong grass, and acid!

– I can take everything but the trip.

– No!

She actually screams it at the bus stop and jumps up and down.

– Monroe!

– You have to take the acid – it's what keeps everyone SMILING!!

– Fucking hell!

The bus pulls up and we get on, it's going to be one of those nights. She tells me one of the guys that is coming out with us tonight is a huge coke dealer and her boyfriend sells stuff too and she's not been back to her parents for who knows how long and she's modelling for a fancy hairdresser in the city and we get off at a big square at Lochend and head to a wee flat in the corner. Her boyfriend is in the living room smoking a big fat joint. He is all jawline and hair. On the sofa, there is a guy completely asleep, face down, hands kind of open – like he is about to be bestowed some kind of gift and he's just waiting for it. He has absolutely no expression. Totally lifeless! He doesn't move at all. Music gets turned up and joints get made and lines are cut and E's popped and hair done and conversations had and the dealer guy turns up and he has white-blond hair to his shoulders and a weird face but he's funny and we do more coke and Monroe begs me to take the trip and the last line answers for me – stick my tongue out!

Then we are gathering cigarettes and skins and keys and the guy on the sofa is still completely motionless.

– Is he breathing?

– Aye!

We all look then head out and maybe he's just gone beyond the need for breath but that would be weird because then he'd be dead and they are sure he's not (I asked) (twice) so he's just a really, really heavy sleeper and there is something about it though, us buzzing all around him, and he doesn't move a muscle but we are in the car by then and coming up fast – tunes on – flying down the M8 to Glasgow, tickets, yes, drugs, yes, hide them in your bra – Jenni? Yes, enough to sell to my guitarist and his pals, yes.

– What age are you?

The dealer turns around in the front and he is gurning like fuck.

– Fifteen.

– Fuck's sake!

He glances at Monroe's boyfriend and they smile in a way that turns my stomach but she is putting her arms around me, super high.

– It's all good, isn't it?

– Aye.

– Everything, Jenni?

– All of it!

– See!

This is issued triumphantly to them and then we float down a queue into the Barrowlands where the Pure DJs kick off, two long screens either side of the stage and a computer-generated dancer on both and a touch of dread in my gut – fear lacing my high – adrenaline taking over. I see my new guitarist and his posh pals and sell them their stuff, then I take some more coke and some more speed and another half E and then I'm in the bathroom and that is where it begins to go wrong.

Always!

Going to the bathroom when really fucking high is – a danger moment.

I am in the club and dancing and the moment and the motion keep me going and even when I am freaking out I'm surrounded by people and then I go into the toilet and close the cubicle door and the muffled bass is just away out there.

– FUUUUCCKKKK!

I am so high.

Too fucked up to sit on the loo.

Shit.

Shit.

Shit.

Shit.

Shit.

This is bad – I'm going to totally freak the fuck out!

Back out.

Clamber along the hallway, arms feeling the way, colours and smoke and then dancers and those screens either side of the stage and I just follow the dancers' moves, just keep dancing, that is how we all survive this, and I can see other people across the room who've taken too much as well and we all just keep dancing – just keep pushing through until this stops. There are glimpses of the dealer and Monroe's boyfriend and she is standing there too with her other friend for a wee while.

– Monroe's acting really strangely tonight!

– Why?

– Dunno.

She is as well, she's stressed out, and I don't want to ever leave this club because when I do I am going to have to go back to that flat with them … it all begins to go in slow motion, hands still in the air – people calling out to the silence, when the music is over.

Lights come up.

Totally drenched in sweat and utterly gutted.

More than that I feel terrified.

Say bye to my new guitarist but I really want to get on the bus that he is on but instead I am in the car with the three of them slick with sweat and eyes like black pennies.

92

We are too high to drive. It is not conjecture, it is a – fact! The dealer jangles the keys.

– How do we do it?

– I don't know, says Monroe.

– Roll a joint, I advise.

– You think?

– Aye, just keep smoking all the way back, we can do it.

It's the dealer guy that is driving.

We float down the motorway with the car about twenty feet up and we are going so slow. If the police see us we are totally fucked.

Monroe leans over to me.

– You'll do whatever I want, ay?

She smiles at them in the front and they are glancing back at us.

My heart drops.

I remember fighting her in Spain, she was the first one to ever get me high and kept me that way (although I liked it) and she didn't listen to what I said when I came back from that guy and here we are in this fucking situation and I have this horrible feeling.

– Come on, say you will!

– Aye, Monroe.

– Aye, she says, ye hear that! Aye, Monroe!

She shoots her hands up in the air and they look back from the front, glance at each other, not a word.

We pull up to the flat.

Go in.

The sleeping guy is still out cold on the sofa. There is a gold-fish swimming in circles in the corner. Didn't notice that before. This music must be doing its nut in. It is swimming around and around. I can't really speak now. They turn the music up. I'm on an armchair so I can see where everyone is in the room. I sit cross-legged. Little Buddha! Monroe switches on this laser and puts her mouth over it like she is sucking cock.

– Always gets the party going, the dealer says.

Bends her head back over and it looks so real, like she really is giving impeccable head to this long blue laser dick. My heart drops. It drops. It drops. It drops. It drops. I know things. It isn't the first time she has done this. She knew this would be happening later on. This show is for them but also it is for me, it's turning my heart to full fear because I knew at some point, when she was jumping up and down saying the acid kept everyone smiling, or in the car, or when the dealer walked in, I knew something was going to go wrong the whole time and I am so high now I can't walk out of here. I am truly a complete fucking idiot.

– Lowering the tone, ay, she's always fucking doing that! Her boyfriend laughs.

She takes the laser deeper into her throat and the guys are loving it. One touches his crotch and there is a bulge there and then the dealer – who is lying on the floor skinning up – turns very deliberately and props himself on his elbow and smiles at me.

– Isn't it a shame there's people like us around – to fuck up a nice young girl like you?

Every hair on my body stands on end.

I am too jaded to go through this shit for anyone and she just keeps sucking the light like it is a cock that will bring her eternal youth and adoration and approval, meanwhile her gross fucking boyfriend is turning around to look at me as well – all three of them waiting now, for me to say something.

– You could try it but you'd have to fucking kill me first.

I say it steady but I mean it, I do.

If they think they are going to fuck my head they have no fucking idea who they are dealing with or what I've already been through.

It wasn't the answer the old cokehead was expecting.

She is shouting something although I could give absolutely no fucks what cos I'd fight the devil himself at this point and then she is blacking out – and it is freaking me out because I know that I will soon too, and it feels like this is something she does every time …

– I'm blacking out!

She's calling it out and he's putting his arms around her.

– It's okay.

– I'm going!

Her hands flounder on the floor, she leans into him.

– It's okay!

Her boyfriend is holding her and the last thing I see is the back of their heads – and I'm gone too.

Things happen when you dream.

Sounds.

Music beats on when you go into that place, the beat is out there and in your heart and in your mind and your brain and it's like we are the music and the room is a play that we are dreaming.

At some point I wake.

Both guys are passed out now.

Monroe hunches over the coffee table like an ancient crone fluttering around with no clue what she is doing. The guy on the sofa is asleep behind her still too. Maybe he is the one who is making all of this happen? Her eyes are lined. She looks old. Like this has aged her and it is taking her looks visibly.

It is daylight outside now, a neon blare of grey-white sun.

– Can you skin up? I can't, she says.

I hold out my hand for the gear and quickly roll two joints and we smoke them in silence, she walks down the hall and I follow her through to the next room where the curtains stay closed all the time – she lies down.

– What the fuck happened? I hiss at her in the dim.

She ignores me and closes her eyes and turns away to go to sleep again. She will not be saying a fucking thing, I know that look. I check over my clothes and I can't tell if they've been put back on but I am wet like I've been in a bath …

– Did you lot put me in a bath?

Nothing.

She is gone.

For hours I lie on the bed next to her like some kid with an unconscious mother who couldn't give a shit. I don't think anyone has fucked me. I would know. I am sure I would know. I don't know why I woke totally soaked though. I sit upright! I knew there was something I had to remember! I am meant to be in court! Like, this morning. Soon! If I don't go to that they won't approve my application to leave the care system. I need to get back to the unit. As I walk down the hall I hear the dealer ask the other one and I think it is entirely for my benefit …

– Is it twisted to make a fifteen-year-old suck your cock?

They are laughing.

I have a feeling that he is saying it to give me an answer about what happened although I don't know if it is the real one or not, he knows fine well I can hear him. Go into the living room and the guy is still motionless on the sofa.

– Is he really alive?

– Think so, aye.

Lick the skins, tighten the joint, poke the end with a Clipper lighter, roll a roach, twist the end, shake it, twist again.

– I knew someone who gave a goldfish an E once, I say.

They look at the goldfish swimming around and then they look back at me.

– What happened to it?

– It swam around and around and around and around and around and then – it died.

– Fuck.

– I need someone to take me home.

– Why?

– I'm in court at 9 a.m.

– Fuck! Really?

It's the coke dealer that drives me in his car, I don't mind him in some kind of weird way, he's honestly what he is, a total cunt, exploitative, but sort of funny with it I guess, you see, the worst kind of cunt is a cunt that doesn't know they are a cunt – the ones that own what they are I have a kind of soft spot for really.

– If you need a job I've got a real high-class place for working girls.

– No thanks.

– You could make great money!

– If I ever go on the game, I won't be giving some guy my fucking money.

I light a cigarette, roll down the window, put my feet up on the dash and he's laughing.

– Oh no?

– No.

– What would you be doing then?

– I wouldn't fuck them either, I'd dress in latex and use whips and chains and shit, you know, fuck them up. I'd hurt them and get paid lots of money to do it. Put it into my own bank account, not fucking yours!

His face lights up and he is clearly in some way charmed by me.

– You ever change your mind, Jenni … call me.

We pull up near the unit and he gives me a card and I float down to the front door and go in and clean myself the fuck up.

93

I can't deal with breakfast so I have three cups of coffee with two sugars in each. That helps. Not much but it helps.

– You look like crap, Jenni!

– I've got a cold.

– Fuck's sake!

My support worker is harassed. He drives. It turns out my old guidance teacher has sent in a reference vouching for my character.

– She says she has filled out the yearbook entry at school for you because you are unable to go into the school and do it yourself.

– They won't have a photo.

– They still want to say something though.

– What?

– The guidance teacher has said – you are the person most likely to surprise everybody.

– What the fuck does that mean?

– Like, in a good way.

– How do you know she meant in a good way?

– I am assuming, Jenni.

– She could have meant I am going to grow up to be a serial killer, or have the first hybrid alien/human baby? I'd do that actually. I would totally have an alien baby.

– I don't think that's what your guidance teacher was thinking.

We pull into a car park and another airless building swallows us in and then we are in a room and there is a woman with an arse for a mouth and a few stooges either side and the chairwoman has seen me before and she's got a look about her this morning. They talk among themselves and act like many of the words are directed to me but they are really not and ten minutes pass, then twenty, and forty.

– You have committed so many crimes …

– Crime is a strong word! my support worker intervenes.

– Look at this list!!

The chairwoman gestures at the paperwork and slides it over to my support worker.

– Aye, well, Jenni has reformed her ways – most of those charges were several summers ago. Six of those are absconding last year which is a waste of police time and resources, that's not really, you know, I mean of course it isn't good but –

The chairwoman cuts my support worker off as she turns to me.

– Do you have anything to say, Jenni?

– No.

– The only reason you are not in a secure unit right now is because you have managed to avoid – countless times now – getting a place there! It is where you should have been the entire time though. We have taken into consideration your references, your recent job, your support from the unit, but it is my opinion that it is only a matter of time before you offend again, in fact you cannot stop yourself, and if you get one – and I mean this – one more conviction, you will go straight to a secure unit until you are sixteen in a matter of weeks, then you will go to a young offenders, and after that I think you will go to prison – which is where I wholly believe you belong. Jenni Fagan, you are a considerable danger – both to yourself and to all of society!

There is spittle around her mouth.

I don't flinch.

Or speak.

Noise is happening, my support worker saying things and they argue but I'm not here.

I'm sitting on a sofa with pigtails.

Long shiny ones.

Imagine!

That would have been so amazing.

I see a little girl with podgy hands. All love. Until they put the light out. Dark box. Floating in space. Gone.

This chairwoman is wrong. I won't get convicted again. I'm going straight. I'll be as poor as a person has to be. I'll clean floors. Or toilets! If I lose my new job I'll do whatever else I have to do to earn money and it won't be from anything other than hard work. If people look down on me then I will take it and I will write, the entire time. I will sing, I will paint, I will find a way to use this energy in me that wants only to destroy and use it to create.

Like the primordial matriarch.

Who created all of desire, all rage, who made all things from that one energy.

94

There is no such thing as clear soup with lemon floating in it. The restaurant is French. It's because my social worker knows I want to go to Paris, actually New York is top of my list, then Paris, then Egypt, then India, then Italy, then Thailand – in reality I'm going nowhere but it costs fuck all to dream. This social worker is young. She's pretty. Dresses well. Seems really smart. Switched on. I like her. She has brought me to a fancy place for lunch for my sixteenth birthday just because she thought it would be nice for me (nothing to do with showing off the chav to her pals) – it's all quite unnerving.

– Sweet sixteen!

– I know!

– So, are you ready for your interview?

– No.

– Do you have any questions about what they are going to ask you, so you can get a chance at this place in homeless accommodation?

– Will they ask me about my record?

– There isn't much they can do, the charges are long-standing, you haven't done anything for at least ten months now, except absconding, and you have a job, right? Your entire record is going to be wiped as of today – when you turn sixteen, all of those convictions are gone forever, you don't need to tell anyone about them. It's a clean slate. Time to start again?

The waiter smiles as I dip my fingers in the clear bowl of hot water with lemon floating in it. Ten minutes ago I told him that I hadn't ordered clear soup. He is happier than a bride as he sees me carefully dry my hands on the napkin (which isn't like the ones in McDonald's where I was taught how to dislodge huge rolls of toilet roll for skint mothers, or the right way to rob Tampax machines). I place the napkin back on the table like I was raised for this fancy shit. The thing is they can't tell. When you look at me off the bat it's pretty uncertain in some ways where I come from. I don't advertise it. I dress different, always did. I don't have any confidence in places like this though. I can hold my own with psychopaths but put me anywhere official or fancy and I close down. Every time I walk in a shop security men always follow me – not cos they think I'm cute and also not cos I steal – I just look guilty – for being alive – and I'm jumpy, I'm on edge, all the time, I wish that I was not.

It's a nice day today.

In my bag there is a pile of books because I've taken out a library card.

– What are you reading?

– All about no wave, new wave, some of the poets, Beats, they called them, and I'm reading *The Color Purple* by Alice Walker fully this time, she is amazing, and this book as well, *I Know Why the Caged Bird Sings* by Maya Angelou – did you know she was once a pimp?

– No.

– Aye, she is amazing but she did that and then, you know, she owned it! You never hear about women doing that. It's okay for Ice-T or Iceberg Slim or Clarence Cooper or someone to say they did all that stuff, or they lived on the streets, or any of it, but not girls, you know, it's not okay for us to say anything.

I don't tell my social worker the other stuff.

I am picking literary mothers and Alice Walker and Maya Angelou are the first two.

I've started reading all these women and about the female punks' lives too because I don't have anyone else to tell me how to be a woman, or a writer.

– Have you seen anyone you grew up with for your birthday, Jenni?

– No.

Don't see anyone now.

I cut out everyone. It means I can go straight. I can write. I can get a room in homeless accommodation hopefully, with a door that has a lock for the first time in my life. I can paint the walls, put candles and plants and flowers and art and second-hand furniture in there and make it really fucking pretty. I already bought myself a stone cherub from my wages. I will give myself the gift of hope for my birthday. I don't tell her about the nightmares or the flashbacks, or that I still check under my bed every single night and I always go to sleep feeling like I'm shrinking to a dot, then disappearing.

95

I had a mother once. I did. I bet she was beautiful. I can't remember anything about her really. I had a brother once. He lives somewhere out there. I hope more than anything that he got a good family and that he is happy. I am struggling. Now I'm a lot straighter there is nothing to keep the memories away. My social worker asked what I thought of the guy that runs our unit. She said there are rumours he is ex-IRA and that he is a controversial figure among the people who work in the care system. I told her he's the best person I have ever met in care because he was able to get through to me when nobody else did, he got me to stop running away just like that. Him and my support worker got me into the office the other day. They shouted at me for a whole afternoon. That I need to wake up. That I can't go around worrying about saving everyone else. That it is going to take all my energy to save myself. That I have something the other kids do not have. That I can't waste it. That I can use my anger to achieve things. That I can use my intellect to do something! They literally kept me in a tiny room and took turns to come in there and shout at me all fucking day like some combination IRA/Foreign Legion shit.

They were really good at it.

When they were done I was on board with everything they were saying.

Except saving other people.

Why wouldn't anyone want to help others even just a little bit?

I left the cool job because it paid nothing and now I get up at 5 a.m. and put on a black knee-length pencil skirt, a white shirt, a rough V-neck jumper in black, tights, a dicky bow tie – and I go clean bins at the burger place at the train station, I have to take them out the back, put new bags in, then I am front-of-house in Wimpy at 6 a.m., cleaning tables of congealed tomato sauce, and even at this time of morning the rent boys are here getting some breakfast before they go home. The ceiling is beautiful in the departures room at the train station. It is round and glass and ornate and so tall and light that pigeons fly up there or they peck their way across the marble floor. Today, there is a piano left out. I have five minutes. Go over. Lift up the lid. Sit down. I used to play the piano for hours and hours and hours and hours. I loved it. Second adoptive family. At her parents'. On every second Sunday. I begged for music lessons but they couldn't afford it. I play a piano song I made up for myself when I was at my adopted grandparents', and I play it over and over and over. Sing quietly. Then a little louder! The board in front of me reads out all the places people can go to. Portsmouth, London, Newcastle, York, Peterborough, Dundee – I want to take a train to Moscow, just to see the buildings there. I love beautiful things so much – they remind me not everything in this world is ugly. Notes on the piano reverb in the domed room. As I close the lid I see him. The bird man! Need to be quick. Gather up my bag and my lighter and sprint for the staffroom door at Wimpy. I can't say how I know the things I know. I do know some things though. Like I had to cut out everyone I ever hung out with if I am to have a chance of being straight. I am choosing to be poor for a long time potentially by leaving a life of easier money, superficially at least. There is no glamour in poverty. It will be hard and it might never end. There will be no thrill, or chance for making money from doing all the wrong things. I am starting with literally nothing and nobody. I also know I am choosing this because when I die the only thing I will take with me – is my soul.

Somehow after all of this it still belongs to me.

I did not lose my shine.

It is literally the only thing I own (that is good) after this absolute fuck-up of a life and so to me it is priceless.

It can't be bought.

So, yes, I can learn to live with nothing!

That's not the worst thing that can happen to me.

It will be fucking brutal but I'm still going to choose it.

If I was to try and keep my little-kid-level dealing and actually build on it then I would have to trade my soul. If you want to survive in that kind of world as a woman then you'd have to be a hundred times more brutal than the men. There are even a few women out there doing it better than men sometimes. It won't be me though.

I'll keep who I am and give myself until I'm forty – to make it in the straight world.

If I don't manage it by then, I'll go back to a life of crime.

That's the deal!

The bird man pauses to feed the birds in the forecourt. It is what he does. He is a long-term homeless gentleman, and he is so mild-mannered, and lovely. All his coats are tattered. He carries countless ancient ripped plastic bags and he has curved fingernails and that isn't why I call him the bird man – it's because he is always feeding the birds in Princes Street Gardens, they flock to him.

I can smell the hot fat in the fryers, the coffee maker and its dense granules, the bins and their pink detergent, the stale cigarettes from the smoking section and there at the front of the counter, where they always are … is the father and the son. The father is eighty-something, and the son is sixty. Both of them dress in their best to come here first thing in the morning (suit jackets, crumpled shirts, trousers, proper shoes, hats) and they are always so happy to see me. If there is a father and a son then there has to be a holy ghost somewhere. I picked up a stone in a witch shop last week and the man there (who told me that he runs twelve covens) said there was so much energy in it from my touch that it burnt him.

I punch in through the staff door.

Charles is there with his glasses and his podgy hands like a sentinel waiting for a first glimpse of me. He is the exact kind of boy that gets a hard-on when he makes a girl cry. He puts his hand up to let me know he is a busy man and I must wait for his attention, ignore that, and behind me comes the bird man, like he does every morning and his layers of coats, his dirty skin, his wobbled gait, his Marks and Spencer's bags all torn, and he places them down and says hello to the father and son who are so happy to greet him because he has been out all night.

Charles sees his moment and leaps to it.

– You can't come in here! he snaps at the bird man.

– Charles. Just leave him alone, okay?

– We don't serve people like you, get out, now – he smells!

This adage is to me – I think Charles is the one who is disgusting, that man is his elder and he is sleeping on our streets and he wants a cup of hot coffee and he's going to fucking get one. People who didn't pay attention to the rules in fairy tales clearly don't know shit. Being humane is the highest form of intelligence. It is the surest proof of a soul. I ignore Charles and pour a hot well-brewed cup of coffee with three creamers and brown sugar while the bird man, the father and the son all watch me.

– Don't you dare!

– Do you want me to start a riot, you little fucking prick?

– This is against company policy –

– Charles, I will deep-fry your fucking spectacles!

– This will cost you your job!

– Fuck off, Charles!

I smile at the bird man and hand him his drink and he takes it with a little smile and no I don't want money and he needs to get out of here and back to streets where he feels less contained by human hypocrisy and I totally understand him on that one. He hobbles out slowly. The father and son nod sagely because justice has been done for the day. Charles is apoplectic and struggling to get his words out.

– I am going to report you!

Off he flounces to see our manager who is some Australian guy who told me he is here because he murdered two people back in his own country and I have to say the work world so far has been weird.

– You know who he is, don't you, Jenni?

The father nods after the homeless man disappearing off to feed birds in Princes Street Gardens.

– No.

– He used to be the manager of the Balmoral Hotel, he was for years, one day he walked out and said he couldn't do it any more, society, the job, all of it, the pressure, the entire thing, he used to wear the smartest suits! He left and he never went back again, his wife and daughter came over from Italy and they tried to get him to come home but he has chosen the streets!

They both look up at me.

– Has the council fixed your windows yet so you can get a heat at home? I ask them.

– No!

Wrinkled socks are exposed under their smartest garb, which still needs mended and cleaned a bit and something about it so touching, the two of them dressed the best they can with suit jackets on and trilby hats to sit here and drink sweet tea and get a heat all day and chat to me, their favourite – so they say.

96

There are no other kids in the unit tonight. I have a stack of books. I will get through this. It's just a day. I'm not Christian. I am pretty sure Santa has a big red line through my name anyway. I wake late and go downstairs. Stoned. It always irritates ginger mullet. He is the one person on today. It is Christmas and I have no fucking presents and nobody loves me and I'm the only freak in here so a tiny little smoke is necessary.

– Is there anything to eat? I ask him.

– Like what?

A smirk along his knobbled jawline.

– I don't know, chicken, potatoes to make roast potatoes, like didn't you even get Christmas lunch?

– There's only one child in here, it would be a waste.

– Is there anything to even make a sandwich?

– Did you not buy yourself something with your food allowance, Jenni?

– No.

– Well, no then.

– Nothing is open!

I need to shut up because every bit of this conversation is giving him nothing but glee. It reminds me of how he was on my little LSD-induced break from reality. I am embarrassed because I never ask for anything but I feel like a piece of absolute nothing right now and he knows it and it is making him so fucking happy.

Upstairs.

Into my room and pick up a book and skin up and skin up and skin up and then sleep.

I wake to black skies and go downstairs barefoot and bleary-eyed.

My support worker is on now and he smiles at me.

– Yer up!

– Is it all over?

– Aye, it's 5 a.m., you slept through it all!

– Thank fuck.

I drop down into one of the office chairs.

– Nearly didn't though, Jen.

– How?

– Mullet was going to phone the police – to get you charged for smoking weed in your room on Christmas Day and, you know, one more charge … that's what the children's court said and they would totally have had you in a secure unit detained for another year. He was in that office picking up the phone to dial the polis when I got in early for my night shift, if he'd have got a hold of them you'd get locked up on Christmas Day and you wouldn't even be able to leave care.

– Why didn't he call them?

– Cos I got him up in a headlock in the hallway and threatened to kick fuck out of him.

Tears.

– You did that fir me?

– Don't look like that, Jenni, fuck's sake, you'll set me off, I did it cos he's a cunt, now let's go out back and have a smoke!

– What??

– You are literally the only kid in care I would ever say that to.

– Why?

– Cos you hate the police more than anyone I've ever met.

We go down the corridor, past the laundry room and out back and we share a smoke and I get him to tell me about his time in the Foreign Legion and his life and I literally beg him to tell me one way to kill a man, just one – so he does, and I get a little something for Christmas that way after all!

97

The staff were told not to have any contact with me when I leave. It's policy. I am allowed to come back and take tins of tuna and stock cubes from the kitchen storeroom though. There was a new woman on last week who I hadn't met before and she just asked me – like it was nothing – if I'd ever been abused in care.

I was so shocked!

– Aye.

– Has anyone ever asked you that before?

– No.

– How long have you been in care, Jenni?

– If you include adoptions, which I do, most of sixteen years.

Turns out if I want to make a complaint about it to the department I have to do so in a court of law. A few days later, she was told to have no contact with me again.

So, I'm leaving care.

I got a place at homeless accommodation, a wee bedsit in the city.

My bedroom in the unit is full of patches where my posters and perfume samples were up and little bits of Blu-tack, and the lovely man who runs this unit bought me a gift of a stop-watch in gold-plated metal because I always wanted one and he thought I should leave with something, he also loaned me some really expensive books on satanism and the occult because I'm studying it but someone nicked them and he wasn't even mad at me, and they know that money I got for furniture is unlikely to be spent on allocated items on the list (spatula from Woolworths?), I have a duvet cover already but I've been using it here and it's seen so many hot rocks it looks like a tea bag – but after this lot of gear I'm stopping it all, I really am, I've had enough. One of the members of staff is going to drive me out to the homeless accommodation in the city and leave me there. I don't have a social worker any more. At some point there will be a homeless officer allocated to me.

There are six bin bags sitting by the front door of the unit.

It is all I have to show for sixteen years.

Nearly thirty moves?

How many names?

All those places.

What I am leaving with after all that is exactly what I arrived with.

I'm leaving care just like I did on the day I left the hospital when I was born.

I have some clothes now and some diaries and my old teddy – Pinky – some photos but that's it, I don't own anything more than this. I take the bin bags to the car outside, put them all in the back seat – climb in beside them.

I don't know at all what's going to happen to me out there – in the real world.

Just like always I won't get to go back – my life in care is over.

From this day on – it's just me.

I'm leaving a life I didn't want to be raised in and it has left its mark all over me. I'm going to make my bedsit so cool, my very first retreat from the world, I'm going to get rag rugs and tea lights that you hang from the ceiling in little cradles and posters and art and I will write there. I will write. I will sing and dance and wear Doc boots and I might finally grow my hair long enough to put it in bunches. I might write to the

Incredible Hulk actor and ask him to sign a photo for me for my bedsit. Look at my little feet – still at the end of my legs, still wearing scuffed boots and going somewhere just like they always were. I have dressed carefully. My heavy lace black dress, tight polo neck underneath, new laces for my Docs; I am wearing lip liner, I painted my nails in French polish even although I am keeping them short enough to learn how to play guitar. It is important to me that I do not look ways I don't want to any more. It's my life now and it is so lonely. The support worker is talking to a member of staff in the door. How many times have I sat in social work cars like this? My heart hurts. The ancestors get in the car beside me. They won't let me leave care and go out into the world like this on my own. They are arguing with each other as ever, which is amusing to me. They are pretty sure where I am going is nowhere near good enough. It's just me and the dead arriving in my first home. I'll doodle out my monsters onto bits of coloured card. Pop them on the shelf. So at night when I'm asleep they can still swim around me. I might not have people right here on this earth to love me and make me safe today of all days but it does not mean I am not beloved. I never told anyone but when I went to the other side when I was twelve they gave me the choice of whether I wanted to come back again or stay there, and I said that I was going to come back even though worse was still to come, even though I knew how hard it would be, but I felt that life is still the only gift we can't waste and that I had something to come back and do. I didn't know what it was yet but I had to have the courage to never stop trying no matter what happened, and they told me, just as I left, to come back to this world, to never forget – those stars up there sparkling so brightly each night, they are shining, just like me.

Epilogue

To choose to live despite fear, or lack of safety, or without so many things, is such a humane thing to do. It is an act of hope. It is love. It is a truth that the human spirit is often so much more than we can understand. I can't say it has all worked out perfectly but I am still here, questioning stories and why people tell them.

The world is full of structures that were built on stories.

Many of those are no longer serving people in any kind of sustainable way, and examining who they benefit, and why, is paramount.

Always look for beauty, especially in the hardest moments.

Sometimes it will be found in nothing more than a snow-drop, or the sky, or the way an old man walks slowly home with his ancient dog and you just know that his companion will not let himself die before him because his owner needs that love.

Every act of goodness, or love, or kindness, counts more than the giver will ever know.

It matters.

I was raised feeling helpless about many things and I watch the world tell us now – that we are almost too far gone in this journey of humanity, that it is nearly too late for the world, our climate, that wars cannot be stopped and individuals will continue to suffer because of injustices that just can't be changed.

Who is telling that story?

This world we are living in is *our* story right now.

It is up to all of us what we want to do with that, and we will pass down our actions, or inactions, to the generations coming after us.

I believe they all deserve so much more.

Words ... are a lighthouse.

They are how we legislate, marry, bury, buy, sell, educate, oppress, control, celebrate, elevate, counter, challenge; the stories we tell are the foundation of what and who we are and they cannot be underestimated.

No good story turns a child away, ever.

I studied families anthropologically as a child and that has continued my whole life.

The ability to scrutinise the ways society interacted with individuals, especially those who did not belong, exposed so much of how the structures we all live within impact on our lives, our deaths, our people, their future.

I questioned the nature of all stories.

When a person in authority, for example, told a story, who did it benefit?

How truthful was it, how fully researched?

I didn't know where I came from, other than I was first admitted onto a psychiatric ward with an unwell mother, at five months in the womb, and I was taken from the hospital on the day I was born. The files couldn't even say where I lived for the first three months of my life. In the end there were up to twenty-seven variations of names, or spellings, and three dates of birth they rotated, and because I knew so very little of my origins, I began to question where humans come from, full stop.

What are we actually doing on this planet?

That existential intensity continued daily from as far back as I remember and the questions really were always the same – what does it mean to live in a universe without a definitive explanation of why we are here, or what happens after we die, or before we are born?

Also, exactly how is an individual's identity formed at all?

We are all told a story about who we are. Often firstly from our families, then schools, newspapers, the legal system, religion, and for many of us those stories are complex and sometimes wholly against our own well-being.

I was raised to observe others' fear, or lack of acceptance, or total inability to see who I was, because they often could not get beyond what I represented as a child in care. Who came from 'those' kinds of people, whose trauma leaked out in behaviours that were solely the expression of all the things I couldn't believe I had to not only hold, but somehow learn to live through.

Those negative projections towards me as a child in care caused as much damage as every other thing I had been through.

Discrimination is a dehumanising act. It deeply compromises the human rights of those who have to reclaim their own sense of self from an overwhelming presence that is often set via political agenda that is actually nothing at all to do with them.

An oppressed group will be profiting another body of people in some way.

Humans have elevated themselves forever as superior, morally, financially, due to ideas of race, or religion, or gender, or sexuality, or any other possible thing that one group of people could think of to gain – at someone else's expense.

I was always suspicious of the motives behind certain stories.

Child abuse is not something that happens only in poor communities, not anywhere near it; it happens in every single part of society, and somehow all of those children are told they are not allowed to ever speak out, let alone own their story, or their own understanding of the things they have been through. They are told they will not be believed, they will be scorned, shamed, belittled, gaslit, attacked or made unsafe.

It is not good enough.

No child should live in fear of anything.

I see people – in politics, or culture, the arts, academia, in police forces, judges, doctors, people who work in prisons, live in prisons, those in custody, those in college, those working so hard to barely make ends meet – carry the generational trauma of their history at great suffering to themselves, and in the worst instances, pass it onto other people after them.

It's time to change the story.

It's time to break the cycles.

It's time to say – this world can do so much better than the superiority, or structural discrimination, the lack of safety, the threats of this bomb and that poverty, the parents watching their kids die from poor mental health, from discrimination, from racism, from homophobia, from religious intolerance, from not being valued – because somebody told a story once saying this person is 'less than', and therefore not worth protecting.

Those stories, and how they impact our legal systems, our education and healthcare systems, alongside personal actions that certain individuals are fairly certain they can get away with ... those stories have made people unsafe, or taken lives from families that should still be here, to be celebrated, to be supported, to be cared for, valued, known.

How extraordinarily lucky was I to have this relationship with words, stories, learning?

To spend my life studying the structures that raised me and find them lacking not just for children like myself, but for everyone; I will say it again, this is *our* story – right now, in this world, at this moment in human history – and we have to change it.

Why don't we write the story where we change the course of human history entirely?

That could be – our story.

Why not?

The only thing any of us are leaving this world with is our soul and the actions we took while alive.

The structures are shaking; it's time to build a foundation that acknowledges and truly learns from what has gone before and what is occurring right now.

What can we give to this life – when we choose to act, even when scared, traumatised, ill, or tired, or demoralised, or weary? I am all of those things, and I have never wanted to tell my story but I am choosing to have more courage because that is a choice, it is an action, and the generation coming behind us right now needs every one of us to be braver and more humane and more vulnerable and more determined than ever to challenge the stories we are being told about everything.

We are living through terrifying times, ideologically, globally, in climate, law, so many different areas, and this world's children, all of them, deserve so much more than the story they are currently being told.

After I had spent my time on the other side, and nearly died, I chose to come back here for a reason. I knew what was going to come would be even harder but I never thought life was meant to be easy.

I believe every other person on this planet has chosen the same.

There is so much work to do.

It begins with words, art, actions, caring.

No act of kindness, defiance, solidarity, caring, courage or sacrifice is meaningless, even when it doesn't get a round of applause or goes unseen – there are so many people carrying extraordinary light throughout their lives, despite all they face, and I am in deep admiration of all of them.

I picked this book up twenty years after I started writing it as a suicide note.

It was waiting.

It took thirty years in therapy, discussing the things in this book, going to legal bodies, creating records of what I have been through, accessing files, seeing my experiences reinforced by what was said in them and totally covered up in others; it took being in pain for decades, endless illnesses, and still being unsafe at times due to never having been taught how to truly value my rights as important; it took seeing my closest people die; it took facing my mortality more times than I wanted to – to decide, to claim my history, my life, my realities, and say I had a right to that voice all along.

I am still here, and I care more than ever.

I live a very specific life, devoted to thinking, studying, writing, making art, going to see what other people are making of this strangest of journeys called a life, and I am knocking on the door of history alongside so many other billions of people – who are all out there, changing the story, for their family, or community, for themselves, or for people they will never even meet.

It's time to change the story.

May you travel well – know beauty, and share the great light of your being.

It is no small act at all.

Author's Note

The research process for *Ootlin* has been rigorous. Firstly, I have kept diaries since I was a child, so recording and studying my own life is something I have always done. I also gained access to my social work files, well over a thousand pages of documentation regarding my life in care. It took me twenty-six years to access the files, only getting them in full when the Freedom of Information Act came in. A lot of the research for my earlier years is taken directly from the files. Some of the instances are just memories that were so impactful I never forgot them and I also had triggers, all my life, around certain things because of those instances. When I was in my early twenties, I first attempted a legal proceeding, reporting what had occurred and is documented in *Ootlin*. Those records are several decades old now.

I have been in therapy for most of the last thirty years, working on all of the subjects in this book. Going over my life so much and keeping diaries all my life proved vital in writing *Ootlin*. I went through another legal proceeding recently in regard to my negative experiences in the care system. I was evaluated over a lengthy period by legal psychologists who verified that in their professional opinion, between my testimony, the recorded history of me dealing with the consequences to my health and well-being, of going through so much child abuse in the care system, also documentation that comes from social work, legal, medical and therapy sources over three decades, everything I raised was true, the consequent lifelong

C-PTSD and fibromyalgia, among various other health issues, being a direct consequence of my childhood.

Finally, I first wrote this book twenty-three years ago when I had only left homeless accommodation four years before that, so my recollection was much more immediate, as was the extraordinary impact it had on my life as an adult. My personal diaries, social work records, therapy from the age of sixteen, and two separate processes reporting my child abuse legally, alongside the original manuscript of this memoir were all valuable sources for research.

If you have been affected by any of the themes in this book, please reach out to:

Who Cares Scotland: www.whocaresscotland.org
Samaritans: www.samaritans.org
NSPCC: www.nspcc.org.uk